CONNECTIONS

The EERI Oral History Series

Clarence R. Allen

CONNECTIONS

The EERI Oral History Series

Clarence R. Allen

Stanley Scott, Interviewer

 Earthquake Engineering Research Institute

Editor: Gail H. Shea, Albany, California
Cover and book design: Laura H. Moger, Moorpark, California

Published by the Earthquake Engineering Research Institute
     499 14th Street, Suite 320
     Oakland, CA 94612-1934
     Tel: (510) 451-0905   Fax: (510) 451-5411
     E-mail: eeri@eeri.org
     Web site: http://www.eeri.org

EERI Publication Number: OHS-10
ISBN (pbk.): 0-943198-20-8
Library of Congress Cataloging-in-Publication Data
  Allen, Clarence R. (Clarence Roderic), 1925-
     Clarence R. Allen / Stanley Scott, interviewer.
        p. cm. -- (Connections: the EERI oral history series)
     ISBN 0-943198-20-8
       1. Allen, Clarence R. (Clarence Roderic), 1925—Interviews. 2. Civil
engineers--California--Interviews. 3. Earthquake engineering—California--History. I.
Scott, Stanley, 1921- II. Earthquake Engineering Research Institute. III. Title. IV. Series.

  TA140.A415.A45 2002
  624.1'762–dc21

                   2002192859

Printed in the United States of America

1 2 3 4 5 6 7 8 09 08 07 06 05 04 03 02

Acknowledgments

The help, encouragement, and editorial feedback of EERI Executive Director Susan K. Tubbesing and the EERI Board of Directors were instrumental in both establishing *Connections: The EERI Oral History Series* and in bringing this volume to publication.

EERI gratefully acknowledges partial funding of this project by the Federal Emergency Management Agency (FEMA).

Table of Contents

The EERI Oral History Series

This is the tenth volume in *Connections: The EERI Oral History Series*. The Earthquake Engineering Research Institute initiated this series to preserve the recollections of some of those who have pioneered in earthquake engineering and seismic design. The field of earthquake engineering has undergone significant, even revolutionary, changes since individuals first began thinking about how to design structures that would survive earthquakes.

The engineers who led in making these changes and shaped seismic design theory and practice have fascinating stories. *Connections: The EERI Oral History Series* is a vehicle for transmitting their impressions and experiences, their reflections on the events and individuals that influenced their thinking, their ideas and theories, and their recollections of the ways in which they went about solving problems that advanced the practice of earthquake engineering. These reminiscences are themselves a vital contribution to our understanding of the development of seismic design and earthquake hazards reduction. The Earthquake Engineering Research Institute is proud to have part of that story be told in *Connections*.

The oral history interviews on which *Connections* is based were initiated and carried out by Stanley Scott, formerly a research political scientist at the Institute of Governmental Studies at the University of California at Berkeley. Scott was active in and wrote on seismic safety policy and earthquake engineering for many years. A member of the Earthquake Engineering Research Institute since 1973, Scott was a commissioner on the California State Seismic Safety Commission for 18 years, from 1975 to 1993. In 1990, Scott received the Alfred E. Alquist Award from the Earthquake Safety Foundation.

Recognizing the historical importance of the work of California's earthquake engineers, Scott began recording oral history interviews with Henry Degenkolb in 1984. Their success let him to consider such interviews with other older engineers. He consulted Willa Baum, Director of the University of California at Berkeley's Regional Oral History Office, a division of the Bancroft Library. Since its inception in 1954, the Regional Oral History Office has carried out and otherwise promoted oral history interviews on a wide range of major subject areas in science and technology, natural resources and the environment, politics and government, law and jurisprudence, and in many other areas. Scott was encouraged to proceed, and the Regional Oral History Office approved an unfunded interview project on earthquake engineering and seismic safety. All of Scott's subsequent interviews were conducted while he was employed by the Institute of Governmental Studies at U.C. Berkeley. Following his retirement from the University in 1989, Scott continued to pursue the oral history project. For a time, some expenses were paid from a small grant from the National Science Foundation, but Scott did most of the work pro bono.

The Earthquake Engineering Research Institute learned of Scott's interview series, and reviewed a number of the early interview transcripts. EERI's interest in preserving these recollections led to publication of this Oral History Series.

In his oral history research, Scott included a selection of senior earthquake engineers who observed and participated in the earthquake safety effort. He included professionals in related fields (geology and geophysics) who also made significant contributions to the body of knowledge in earthquake engineering. His research efforts document much of the early evolution and milestone events of the profession.

Stan Scott passed away in January 2002. He leaves a legacy of nine published volumes and eleven additional finished interviews (Scott left his archives to EERI). This, the tenth volume, is the first since Scott's death last winter, and EERI will publish the remaining interviews in future volumes of *Connections*. EERI, and indeed the entire structural engineering profession, is indebted to Scott for his tireless efforts. He single-handedly created an important historical archive of earthquake engineering history since the 1920s—hundreds of hours of taped interviews, thousands of pages of transcripts. Were it not for Scott's interest in earthquake engineering history and how it developed, his diligence, and his devotion to seeing these memories preserved, these recollections would be forgotten and lost.

The Earthquake Engineering Research Institute was established in 1949 as a membership organization to encourage research, investigate the effects of destructive earthquakes and the causes of building failures, and bring research scientists and practicing engineers together to solve challenging engineering problems through exchange of information, research results, and theories. In many ways, the development of seismic design is part of the history of EERI.

EERI Oral History Series

Henry J. Degenkolb	1994
John A. Blume	1994
Michael V. Pregnoff and John E. Rinne	1996
George W. Housner	1997
William W. Moore	1998
Robert E. Wallace	1999
Nicholas F. Forell	2000
Henry J. Brunnier and Charles De Maria	2001
Egor P. Popov	2001

Future Subjects

L. LeRoy Crandall	Clarkson W. Pinkham
Roy G. Johnston	Earl Schwartz
Ralph S. McLean	George A. (Art) Sedgewick
John F. (Jack) Meehan	James Stratta
Joseph P. Nicoletti	William T. Wheeler

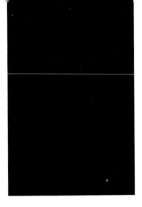

Foreword

Most of my oral history interviews have been with structural engineers, the only exceptions being senior-statesman-geologist Robert Wallace of USGS, who contributed to seismic safety methodology and policy in very significant ways. This volume features geophysicist Clarence Allen of Caltech, who also has been a major contributor to the art and science of earthquake engineering and the cause of seismic safety. In addition to his own teaching and research, Allen's professional life has been filled with geophysical consulting work world-wide, as well as distinguished lectureships and an array of awards, including two specifically related to seismicity and seismic safety: the first G.K. Gilbert Award in seismic geology, given in 1960 by the Carnegie Institution of Washington, D.C., and the Alfred E. Alquist Award, given in 1994 by the California Earthquake Safety Foundation.

I had known Clarence since the late 1960s, from my early days of working with Karl Steinbrugge and others who were helping Senator Alfred E. Alquist's Joint Legislative Committee on Seismic Safety. Over subsequent years, I was to encounter him often, especially at EERI conferences and in committee work for the Seismic Safety Commission. Then in the early 1990s when interviewing George Housner at the Atheneum I would often see Clarence when he came there for lunch. When I neared the end of the Housner interviews, I asked Clarence if I might have a few oral history sessions with him. He agreed, and these interviews are the result. I believe they will make a very significant addition to the EERI Oral History Series.

This oral history is based on four interviews with Clarence Allen, recorded in 1995 and 1996. All the interviews were held in the Atheneum, the faculty club on Caltech's campus in Pasadena. Subsequently, he and I edited the transcript, which he also revised and updated with new information. The last revisions were made in 2001, a few months before publication.

Stanley Scott
(November 1, 1921–January 5, 2002)
Research Associate
Institute of Governmental Studies
University of California, Berkeley

Personal Introduction

I was first introduced to Clarence Allen in 1965 through a common colleague, the late James L. Sherard, an internationally respected engineering consultant and one of the early principals of Woodward-Clyde-Sherard and Associates. The 1964 Alaska earthquake had shaken loose some apprehension in Sacramento, causing Clarence and Jim to be appointed members of one of the first scientific and engineering groups charged with advising the State of California on the studies needed to better understand its earthquake threat. I served as Jim's alternate on this committee, and had the opportunity to meet and work with both Clarence, who became chairman of the scientific coterie, and George Housner, the chairman of the engineering component. I can tell you, I felt very fortunate to be in the company of such distinguished scientists and engineers.

At about that time, Jim Sherard was in the process of writing a new edition of his textbook on the siting, design, and construction of earth and rockfill dams.[†] He was troubled with the inability of the scientific community to come to some consensus on assessing earthquake hazards for the safe siting and design of dams and other important facilities. Jim came to know and respect Clarence Allen's ability to explain accurately what the scientific community knew and, more important, did not know about earthquakes and their effects. He discovered then what we all now know: Clarence is a wonderful writer and speaker. One of Clarence's admirable traits is the way he shares his knowledge so clearly, articulately, and often with humor.

The next time I ran into Clarence, I was in the field investigating the 1966 Parkfield, California, earthquake with Karl Steinbrugge, Gordon Oakshott, and Burt Slemmons. We were tracing the surface fault rupture through the fields near Parkfield and across Highway 46, where the yellow line in the center of the road was displaced. This is where we met Clarence Allen. As we shook hands, Clarence said, "Hello, Ray." I was devastated! It was some time before I realized that Clarence had my name confused with that of the prominent earthquake engineer Ray Clough—not a bad person to be confused with!

When Clarence decided to pursue his doctorate in geophysics at Caltech, he chose to study the San Andreas fault in the San Gorgonio Pass area, southeast of San Bernardino. His experience as a B-29 navigator during World War II exposed him to the fascination of observing terrain and geology from the air, and navigating from maps. This combination, I suspect, resulted in his Ph.D. being mostly a geologic treatise.

[†] James L. Sherard, *Earth and Rock-fill Dams: Engineering Problems of Design and Construction*. 1963.

To this day, when you travel by air with Clarence, you learn that he always chooses a window seat and frequently carries his air navigation maps. He gets annoyed when seatmates want the window shades closed, because he wants to watch the geology go by. At anytime during the flight, he can tell you exactly where the plane is by observing the geology and knowing the regional geologic relationships, almost anywhere in the world.

Clarence has published extensively. Many of his papers have had an influence on the evolution of the theory of plate tectonics, and several have become classics that are referenced extensively in the worldwide literature. His BSSA publication in 1965 on the relationship of seismicity and geologic structure in southern California taught many about the direct relationship between geology and seismicity[††].

His 1975 Geological Society of America Presidential Address, "Geologic Criteria for Evaluating Seismicity," published in 1976 in the GSA Bulletin, was a classic. That paper and his earlier work set the stage for the development of a relatively recent scientific discipline, paleoseismology. Through the evolution of new investigative thinking and techniques, paleoseismology has allowed a more complete, accurate, and realistic understanding of long-term earthquake occurrences.

Clarence's book, "The Geology of Earthquakes," Oxford University Press, 1997 (co-authored with Robert S. Yeats and Kerry Sieh), I believe, is the most important book written about the intimate relationship between earthquakes and geology. It is a must-read for geologists, engineers, and anyone interested in a practical understanding of earthquakes and the tectonic processes that cause them.

One of the most fascinating aspects of Clarence's career is his leadership in and influence on the field of earthquake prediction. In 1975, the growing prospects for earthquake prediction, based in part on the tentative experience of the Chinese, Japanese, and the Soviets, suggested that a capability to predict earthquakes had been or was being developed. The Chinese claimed to have predicted the February 1975 magnitude 7.3 earthquake in Haicheng, China, when the Chinese government evacuated one million people shortly before the occurrence of the quake, saving perhaps hundreds of thousands of lives.

[††] Allen, C.R., St Amand, P., Richter, C.F., and Nordquist, J.M., "Relationship between Seismicity and Geologic Structure in the Southern California Region," *Seismological Society of America Bulletin*. Vol. 55, 1965.

Until the mid-1970s, the United States did not have an earthquake prediction program. The President's science advisor assisted in forming a panel of experts to advise the National Science Foundation and the U.S. Geological Survey in addressing not only earthquake predictions, but also earthquake hazard assessments and engineering methods to mitigate the damage. During 1975 and 1976, Clarence and I were members of this group, which was known as the Newmark-Stever Panel on Earthquake Prediction and Hazard Mitigation. The panel's report, which Clarence had a large part in writing, contributed to creating the National Earthquake Hazard Reduction Program that passed into law in 1977.

In 1980, Clarence was chairman of the U.S. National Earthquake Prediction Council, and was invited to an International Seminar on Earthquake Prediction, in San Juan, Argentina. During the mid-1970s, two U.S. scientists had developed what they believed to be a reliable earthquake prediction technique and predicted a great earthquake (magnitude 8.5+) offshore from Lima, Peru. Such a large earthquake, if it were to occur, would have catastrophic consequences. This prediction was a major topic at the seminar in San Juan.

Upon his return to Pasadena, Clarence attended a media reception at the NASA Jet Propulsion Laboratory. During the dinner that followed, Clarence, believing the Peru prediction had been made public, related stories about his trip and the "Brady-Spence prediction." The reporters in attendance, eagerly listening, immediately sensed a spectacular headline. Within a few days, major news stories appeared: "Scientists Predicting Peru Quake," Boston Globe, November 9, 1980; "Great Quakes Predicted for Peru," Miami Herald, November 10, 1980; "Huge August Earthquake Predicted for Peru and Chile," New York Times, November 16, 1980. As one of the reporters later explained, "Earthquake prediction stories from South America are discountable, but Clarence Allen talking about a prediction is news."

Clarence's leadership resulted in a shift away from earthquake predictions that profess to say exactly when the "big one" will strike; such predictions are still in the throes of adolescence. He realized it was of greater value to study where and how large the inevitable temblor would be, and to prepare for it.

What Clarence Allen said carried a lot of weight with those in the public policy arena, as well as the scientific and engineering communities. When it comes to understanding earthquake hazards and how to deal with the related risks, Clarence is one of the most accomplished, honored, and distinguished scientists in the earthquake world. He is particularly adept at integrating the interdisciplinary fields of geology, seismology, and geophysics to achieve accurate and reliable estimates of earthquake potential and related effects, as well as communicating that knowledge to engineers and decisionmakers.

I have been very fortunate in my career to have been associated with Clarence during the past 30 years. We have worked together as consultants and advisors on numerous projects; some of the major ones have included the Seismicity Evaluation and Seismic Safety Assessment of the Bolivar Coast Dikes in Venezuela, 1968; the proposed Auburn Dam in California, 1977; the Seismic Safety Evaluation of the Proposed Liquefied Natural Gas Terminal at Point Conception, California, 1982; the Seismic Safety Evaluation of the Aswan High Dam in Egypt, 1986; and the Seismic Safety Reevaluation of the Diablo Canyon Nuclear Power Plant, California, 1991.

As a geologist, Clarence's reputation has no bounds. In 1997, I participated in a reconnaissance along most of the length of the Anatolian fault, in Turkey. During our concluding meeting in Istanbul, we had dinner with a Turkish professor who is well known for expressing his opinions on matters geological and otherwise. During the dinner discussion, I asked the professor if he knew Clarence Allen. He enthusiastically described Clarence as a fine scholar and a gentleman, then shouted loudly above a noisy crowd, "most of all, Clarence Allen is one damned good geologist!"

Clarence R. Allen has credibility. Credibility is about having earned the trust, respect, and confidence of colleagues and friends. As you read Clarence's story that follows, it is clear that Clarence's family history and his family relationships have had a direct and profound influence in shaping his character. When you disclose your history, you disclose your values.

Scientific imagination, enthusiasm, integrity, honesty, and openness also characterize Clarence Allen. He has intellectual capital and a quick wit. Clarence enjoys good food and wine, is a wonderful cook, and an ardent stamp collector. I am proud to be able to call Clarence my friend.

Lloyd S. Cluff
Manager, Geosciences Department
Pacific Gas & Electric
San Francisco, California

CONNECTIONS

The EERI Oral History Series

Clarence R. Allen

Chapter 1

Early Years and Family Background

There were important early influences that disposed me to like the kinds of things a field geologist does . . . my father used to enjoy travelling and camping out with the family . . .

Scott: Before we talk about your professional background, let's talk a little about your family and your early background.

Allen: My grandfather, Edward Allen, on my father's side came here to Pasadena in 1885, and my father was born here in 1895. My coming back to Pasadena and Caltech in 1949 is, however, unrelated to that, inasmuch as all my family had left Pasadena by that time. I was actually born in Palo Alto, California, in 1925, when my father, Hollis Allen, was in graduate school at Stanford, studying school administration. For at least part of that time, my parents and older brother were evidently living in a tent in what is now Menlo Park, where they had set up housekeeping among the oak trees. I know my father often regretted that he had not bought some property there, had he been able to.

Earlier, my father had served in World War I as an aerial armaments officer. He had started at Pomona College before the war—supporting himself on various odd jobs—and finished in 1918 following his wartime service. He then took advantage of his interest and work experience in mechanics to obtain a teaching credential at the normal school in Santa Barbara, which subsequently became the University of California at Santa Barbara. He was credentialed to teach "machine shop, sheet metal, mechanical drawing, cabinetmaking and woodworking, blacksmithing, auto mechanics, foundry, pattern-making and electrical work"!

His first full-time school job was teaching blacksmithing and mechanics at Pomona High School, some 30 miles east of downtown Los Angeles. From there, in 1922 he moved to Big Pine, California, up in the Owens Valley, to be school superintendent. My brother was born there, and we often considered it our family home because my mother and father had so much enjoyed the small-town life, the people, and the local environment of the Owens Valley. My family was there during much of the controversy over the Owens Valley Aqueduct. My father took the 1924-1925 school year off to obtain his master's degree in education at Stanford University, and it was during this stint that I was born.

I am not sure when my father went to San Bernardino, but it must have been around 1927, because the eldest of my sisters, who was two years younger than I, was born there. He became assistant superintendent of schools there. From San Bernardino he was called to the Claremont Graduate University, then called the Claremont Graduate School, in

about 1929 as the first full-time professor of educational administration, and where he spent most of his professional career. People who become professors of education do not usually start out teaching blacksmithing! He was very proud of that background, however, and was always very adept at doing things mechanical. He passed some of that on to his children. He took time off from the Claremont job to complete his doctorate work at Stanford in 1934.

I went from kindergarten through the 12th grade in Claremont, except for a couple of years in Boston that I'll talk about presently. Since my father was a teacher, we often had time off in the summer for trips. We used to take a lot of automobile trips, travelling in our old 1927 Dodge and camping out. We went all over the West, and across the continent a couple of times. As a result, I became very interested in things geographical and learned to enjoy working with maps. I think the fact that I am in the earth sciences today reflects this early background and interest.

My mother died when I was in the sixth grade. It was a very traumatic experience for the family. Her death was from some sort of heart complication shortly following the birth of my youngest sister, and my father was left with four kids. Obviously this was difficult for him, but only later, in retrospect, did I realize how very difficult that was. My aunt came up from Mexico to help with the family during that time.

But then my father was called to Harvard University, where he became director of the summer session in education and in charge of teacher placement. So I did my first two years of junior high school in Massachusetts. This must have been 1937-38, because I missed the

1938 flood, and in fact regretted not being in Claremont when that happened. But we four children were basically rather unhappy there in Massachusetts. We were used to the West, and not being able to wear Levi's to school was a big issue with my brother and myself. A move like that and especially under those circumstances would have been a traumatic experience for us in any event.

Although he had a great future before him at Harvard, my father decided to come back to California—again to the Claremont Graduate University. Only recently have I realized what a kudo it was to be called from a place like Claremont to a very responsible position at Harvard. I think he came back to Claremont primarily because of his children. While he also enjoyed it here in California, and he also had some misgivings about the smugness of the Harvard environment, I think the happiness of the kids was the critical factor for him.

Scott: The children's happiness must have been very important to him if that was the principal reason he came back.

Allen: I think so. Anyway, along with my brother I completed high school in Claremont. My youngest sister was about ten years younger than I. We continued to do a lot of travelling, and then some few years later, maybe five or so, my father remarried. My stepmother, Janet, became a very integral part of the family.

I can say that basically, at least from my perspective, our family life was very pleasant. Some people seem to have bad memories of certain aspects of their childhood, but I have always looked back on mine as a pleasant experience, despite a couple of traumatic years following my mother's death. In high school I particularly enjoyed the science classes, which I thought were the most challenging ones. It was sort of a macho thing to do—trying to take the hard things. My math teacher, William W. Booth, a Caltech graduate, was one of the very best teachers I ever had.

Grandparents on Both Sides

Scott: Who were your grandparents? Where did they come from?

Allen: On my mother's side, the family members were Congregational missionaries. Her father, Alfred Clarence Wright, was a missionary among the Yaqui Indians in Mexico. My mother, (Alfreda) Delight Wright, was born in El Paso, but at the time the family was living in Chihuahua. My grandfather used to tell very interesting stories about the Yaqui Indians, who were not, at least at that time, the most friendly people, and about trying to Christianize them. My mother's brother was a preacher, and her sister later operated a missionary school in Guadalajara, Mexico. The family had a real church background—was very strongly church-oriented.

My grandfather on my father's side, Edward Bernard Allen, was born in Massachusetts. He learned a trade as a bookbinder, but at the age of 22 decided to try his fortunes in California, where the family evidently had some friends in Pasadena he initially stayed with. He had a little money, and he persuaded some others to join him in investing in real estate during the great booms and busts in the real estate market here.

All of that money was lost, so in the ensuing years he worked as a farm laborer, a surveyor, and church janitor, to pay back those to whom he felt indebted. He was also a skilled carpenter, and over the years built many houses in Pasadena, a number of which still stand today. Sometime shortly after the turn of the century, he bought a small towel-supply business for $200, and this grew into his primary occupation during the remainder of his working career. I remember my father telling of working after school each day in delivering clean towels to various institutions in Pasadena, at first by bicycle and later by horse-drawn wagon. My grandfather was a very hard worker with a strong work ethic, which he passed on to his children—and hopefully even to his grandchildren. I recall that at age 75, after he had retired and moved to Claremont to be near his children, he hired another carpenter, and they together built a small house in which he resided until his death some years later!

My grandfather Allen met and married a woman who was in the second graduating class at the University of Southern California (USC). So, while he had no collegiate education at all, my grandmother did. Also, despite their devastating losses and very modest income afterward, they ended up sending all four of their children through college. I think that each of the children essentially had to work his or her own way through college, but they were certainly inspired by parental influence. As I mentioned earlier, my father went to Pomona College. In fact, my father and mother met at Pomona College, which then—more than now—was a Congregational school. A lot of children of Congregational missionaries

were there. Pilgrim Place in Claremont is still a home for retired church workers, many of whom were missionaries.

Missionary Connections and Interest in Geography

Allen: One of my father's sisters went to China as a missionary, and spent almost her whole career there. She later got out of China in quite an adventure, just as the Japanese were coming in—I believe in the early 1940s. She lived with our family in Claremont for several years, and eventually went to Pilgrim Place. So on both sides of my family there are missionary backgrounds, and this also increased my interest in geography.

Scott: Those missionaries got around to all kinds of places.

Allen: Yes they did. I visited my aunt who ran a school in Guadalajara, Mexico, and had correspondence with the aunt who was in China. Also my missionary relatives had other missionary friends. My grandfather also started a stamp collection, which I still have. There is nothing like stamp collecting to get you interested in geography. In those days there were so many places that do not exist now—at least under those names—such as Togoland, German East Africa, and other places you never hear about any more.

He actually had a pretty good stamp collection, except that he wanted to make all the stamps look prettier. So he took scissors and cut off the perforations, which of course reduced their value to essentially zero. Otherwise we would have some early U.S. stamps in that collection that would really be worth something. I kept up that interest in stamp collecting, and my brother was also involved in it while he was in high school. I have not done much since World War II, except try to refurbish the collection. As I understand it, in the postwar period, no stamps are worth very much—unless you are interested, say, in the artwork—because they are printed in such large numbers. But with the missionary connections, the stamp collection, and those kinds of influences, we heard a lot about foreign places. I had maps and globes and was always interested in various parts of the world.

While my father and mother were religious people, they were not as much so as their parents had been. Particularly after my mother died, my father was not a strongly religious person, not in the sense that I suspect his parents would have wished him to be. He did, however, have a very strong sense of Christian ethics and morality, and his parents were very happy with his choice of education as a career.

Early Influences

Allen: There were important early influences that disposed me to like the kinds of things a field geologist does, although I had hardly heard the term "geology" at that time. For one thing, my father used to enjoy travelling and camping out with the family, so we took many trips when I was in grammar school and high school. I remember one trip when I was very young, probably about 1930, when I would have been five. My mother's brother, who was also a minister, was teaching Spanish at the University of Oregon. We decided to visit him and his family up there.

For that trip, my father was determined to drive in our 1927 Dodge from Claremont to

Eugene, Oregon, without ever getting on a paved road. That was his objective, reflecting I guess his interest in places off the beaten path. Moreover, he actually did it. We left Claremont, going over the mountain—at that time you could use some of the Forest Service roads and get across the mountains in the Baldy area. We went out through the desert into Nevada. Then we went up through western Nevada, all the way up into Oregon. Finally we went across one of the passes over the Cascades and reached Eugene. We essentially did go all the way to Eugene without getting on a paved road, and camping the whole way.

Scott: Your father liked to see the back country.

Allen: Yes, he liked to see the back country. He himself had lived in Big Pine and enjoyed the remote country and the people he met there. But that experience represents some of the influence that got me interested in getting around in different kinds of terrain.

I should also mention the Boy Scouts, another strong influence that got me subsequently interested in going into the earth sciences. My Boy Scout experience in the late 1930s and the early 1940s was important in that connection. At that time it was a very different kind of organization from what it is now. Back then, the Boy Scouts were very much oriented toward outdoor activities. You got merit badges for lighting fires without matches and that sort of thing, along with athletic-related activities. Nowadays, of course, the emphasis of the Boy Scouts has necessarily changed a good deal.

Essentially, the whole reason for the existence of the Boy Scout troop that I belonged to in

Claremont was for going camping. We used to plan camping trips, some of them backpacking trips. You develop many friends in this way, and it was a lot of fun. While I never became an Eagle Scout—I only reached a Star or something like that—it certainly helped shape my interest in the outdoors.

Scott: Would you say a little more about that?

Allen: I remember one day, when we were living in Claremont, my brother and I decided we would climb Ontario Peak, which is the 8,700-foot peak just northeast of Claremont. We were going to spend the night in a little campground at what is now Mt. Baldy Village. It turned out to be the first snowstorm of the season, and my brother and I struggled up through the snow and ice to the top of the peak, and then finally got back down to the campground nearly frozen, and eventually got a fire going and made dinner. My father was determined not to interfere, but he did drive by somewhat surreptitiously to make sure that we had gotten back to the campground, although he did not dare tell us that he was checking up on us.

I also remember a trip we took in 1938, when my brother and I, plus a high school friend of his, went backpacking in the Sierra Nevada, in what is now Kings Canyon National Park. In those days, backpacking was a different matter from what it is now. Back then, just trying to find a pack was rather difficult. Also, there were no packaged foods specially prepared for backpacking. I don't think we even had sleeping bags, but carried blankets.

Also, we did a fair amount of fishing. My father had a telescoping steel rod, and we occasionally went fishing with him around Claremont. There was good fishing in the area back then. In San Antonio Canyon there was a beautiful little brook coming down through the trees. There was also another trout-filled stream over near what is now Rancho Cucamonga. Then my brother and I also did quite a bit of fishing in the Sierra Nevada. At that time there were fish everywhere, and you could not help but catch fish, even with a very crude fly. We were fly fishing, not bait fishing. We had done the fishing partly to maintain our food supply when in the Sierra, and we had even caught rattlesnakes and ate some of those, to help vary the diet a little.

I was never really an avid fisherman as a kid, however, and later I essentially dropped it completely, until some 30 years ago, when I took up trout fishing again to get out of the office and get a little exercise. While I am not really a mountain climber, and certainly not adept at true rock climbing, I have enjoyed backpacking into various areas with friends and colleagues. I essentially had developed that interest clear back when I was in junior high school and in the early years of senior high school—hiking in the local mountains.

More recently, I have done a lot of fishing, with the exception of the last couple of years. Bob Sharp of Caltech and I, along with some other friends, have backpacked into all four corners of Yellowstone Park on fishing trips. Partly as a result of these trips, Sharp finally decided to build a house—a summer home—just outside the northeast entrance to Yellowstone Park. Since he built his house, I have been up there several times fishing for a week or two. From his very early days Bob was a fisherman, a trait he also inherited from his father.

I also did a lot of fishing with Paul Jennings, my Caltech engineering colleague, here in the local southern California area, where there is much better trout fishing than most people ever dreamed of. Some of these little streams here have some remarkably good fishing. Also, Paul and I have been to New Zealand fishing twice, and I have had the opportunity to fish in South America, the Himalayas, and so forth.

I was always intrigued by the fact that trout fishing and earthquakes seemed to go together. The fact is that trout are particularly abundant in cold-water streams, typically in mountainous areas such as the Andes or the Himalayas. Mountains are there because of tectonic processes, among which are earthquakes. In almost all areas the Europeans ever got to, the higher mountains have been stocked with trout. So it was obvious why I so often found good trout fishing in the places where I went to do field studies of earthquakes. These are the same kinds of areas where trout are likely to be found.

Scott: Tectonic processes produce uplift, and this in turn means more precipitation—rain and snow—and streams to carry the cold water downhill.

Allen: Yes. Trout generally require cold water, which typically comes with altitude in most parts of the world. For example, in Venezuela I was working in the Mérida Andes at high elevations, although most of the country is in the jungles where there are certainly no trout—lots of piranhas but no trout. In the Mérida Andes, however, there is some wonderful trout fishing.

On the other hand, Bob Sharp, who was once one of my professors and who has been a colleague now for many years, warned me about mixing geology and trout fishing in practice, at least on the same day: "When you are going out to do geology, you do not carry a fly rod. You have to do one or the other—you cannot pretend that you are going to do both on the same day." Bob Sharp was right—if you are going to do geology, you'd better not be dreaming of switching to fishing at five o'clock.

Other Early Predispositions to Field Geology

Allen: These are some little vignettes of some interests I developed early, and that made field geology a good career choice later. I feel very lucky to have been able to find a profession that involves so many of these activities that I like and have been interested in. Again, I think this comes from my father, who just enjoyed doing the practical stuff. I remember he had a machine gun from World War I. He was an aerial armaments officer in World War I, and when he left he had a machine gun with several belts of ammunition. I remember working on that thing night and day with my father. We finally went up into the wash north of Claremont to try to get the gun to work. We did get it to fire single shots.

When World War II came, we gave it to the Claremont civilian defense department, and that was the last we saw of it. Also, because my father had been an armaments officer, I was interested in guns to a modest degree. I remember as a kid doing lots of target practice with a .22 rifle. During my service in World War II, I qualified as an expert on the Thompson submachine gun, the Colt .45, and the carbine. But I suspect that today I could not hit that table over there. I don't think that I have fired a gun since World War II, and I tend to be very pro-gun-control today.

Something else from my high school days that got me interested in travel and exploration was the 1937 movie "Lost Horizon," with its tale of Shangri-La. It starred Ronald Colman, Jane Wyatt, Sam Jaffe, and Edward Everett Horton, based on the book by James Hilton. It was directed by Frank Capra, who, incidentally, was a Caltech graduate. Somehow the fantasy of that movie intrigued me, and one reason I later chose to work in Tibet was to see some of that fantasyland.

In subsequently reading Hilton's book I discovered some interesting things that were not in the movie. An example is when Conway left Shangri-La with his brother and his brother's girl friend—who was soon to turn 200 years old. The brother and fiancee both die, but Conway struggled on to survive. Much of the movie photography for those scenes was done in the Alps, and it was just fantastic. Conway finally arrived at a little place on the edge of Chinese civilization called Tatsien-Fu. While almost everything else in the book was imaginary, Tatsien-Fu (now known as Kangding) is a real place that still exists, and I have been there several times. It is a little town in westernmost Szechuan on the border between the areas populated by the Han people of China and the Tibetans.

Shangri-La was supposedly hundreds of miles west of there. In fact, that is an area where I have worked, although I have not yet found Shangri-La. One of the last lines in the movie was after Conway had decided he wanted to try

to return to Shangri-La, and people kept pursuing him, but kept missing him. He disappeared into the wilderness and they never caught up with him again. The final scene was at the Embassy Club in London, where Lord Gainsford, who had just returned from the futile chase of Conway back into Tibet, proposed a toast: "Here's my hope—that Robert Conway will find his Shangri-La. Here's my hope that we all find our Shangri-La." Anyway, I was intrigued by that fantasy, and it certainly increased my desire to see some of the odd, forbidden places of the world. And I have had great opportunities to do that in many places, including Tibet.

Siblings

Scott: Before you leave the discussion of your family, would you say a little more about your siblings, whom you have mentioned several times?

Allen: There were four of us—two brothers and two sisters. My brother, Roland, who is two years older than I, was born in Big Pine. He always wanted to be a cattle rancher. I remember my mother patting him on the head and saying, "Yes, yes, you'll be a cowboy." But he really is a cattle rancher! He studied animal husbandry at Cal Poly in San Luis Obispo. Then after he finished with World War II, being very independent-minded and fed up with government subsidies, he refused his mustering out pay, bought a Model A Ford, and then ran out of gas in a town called Panguitch, in southern Utah. He lived there for many years—probably one of the only non-Mormons in town—and starting out as an auto mechanic, he then gradually managed to buy cattle.

Finally he got to the point where he could subsist entirely from what he made from the cattle ranching. He ran cattle in the Glen Canyon area, then way out in the boondocks.

I visited his range once, and think we had to ride a day on horseback even to get to the edge of it. He has maintained his cattle ranching ever since. He married and subsequently moved, and now runs cattle out of Glenwood, New Mexico. He is now well over 70 years old, but wants to die with his boots on. [Allen's brother died in April 2001, subsequent to final revisions on this manuscript, and with his boots on.] Every night he reads like mad, and is far more up on current events than I am. He is really an intellectual, but is also one of these guys who worships manual labor. You no doubt have known people like this—who think that anyone who is not doing manual labor is somehow sinning.

Scott: Yes. I grew up in a farming community in Texas, and later my father had a small ranch in New Mexico. Manual labor was really a way of life back there, as well as a livelihood.

Allen: Although, like many cattlemen, my brother is somewhat conservative in his politics, he is not completely so by any means. Like many cattle people, he is quite vociferously anti-environmentalist. He jokingly says there is only one thing he dislikes more than Sierra Club members, and that is Californians in general. Of course, he grew up here in California. Anyway, he is a very interesting character.

Scott: Most of the cattle people I have known grew up on a ranch or a farm, or had some very close connection with that kind of life.

Allen: Yes. If you do not inherit a ranch or a fortune, it is very difficult to get into the field. When my brother was first in Panguitch, he was living with some people who were running cattle, and they helped him along. He was able to get into it gradually. He was always on government land—with either Taylor grazing permits or Forest Service grazing permits.

He enjoys his work no end. You could not get him to come to Los Angeles now. He came here once about 30 years ago and was so scared by the freeways that he said "Never again!" When we grew up in Claremont we were out in the orange groves. But he did go to college, at least for a couple of years at San Luis Obispo, and the animal husbandry he took at Cal Poly furthered his interest in that area. It certainly helped him along when he eventually did get into working with cattle.

My brother was a conscientious objector at the start of World War II. He joined the American Field Service as an ambulance driver and ended up in the Near East, where he saw a lot of combat action during the North African battles, such as at El Alemain, against German general Erwin Rommel. Then, after a couple of years of very difficult and dangerous service, he decided that he was no longer a conscientious objector and enlisted in the U.S. Army in Egypt. When he left the Army and ambulance driving, however, his biggest skill was in auto mechanics. He had developed that well before he went into the service. He and I owned several Model T and Model A Fords.

Scott: Those needed to be worked on often and sometimes almost reconstructed. It was a good way to learn auto mechanics.

Allen: That's right. I remember one Model T in which my brother and I and one of our school teachers decided to drive to San Francisco for the World's Fair Exposition on Treasure Island, in 1939. When we started out, we got as far as Tarzana, about 50 miles, before the first rod went. We spent all night under the car getting the rod replaced. Then we got as far as Gaviota, up past Santa Barbara, probably another 120 miles along the way, where another rod went out, and we spent a lot of time on that. Then a main bearing went out at King City, about 150 miles short of San Francisco.

So we sold the Model T for junk for $5.00 and hitchhiked on up to San Francisco. We found some friends to come back with on the return trip. At any rate, my brother became a very skillful mechanic then and while he was in the ambulance service. When he was out of the service, he had no trouble finding work as an auto and heavy equipment mechanic, but he did not want to do that for life. So he has successfully gotten into the cattle business.

My sister Connie, two years younger than I, graduated from Pomona College and became a teacher. Her husband was a professional photographer with a job in the San Fernando Valley. They lived in Pasadena, and she was a school psychologist in the Walnut area. Then she developed multiple sclerosis, which took her out of teaching. Fortunately, however, she has been on somewhat of a plateau ever since. She is still alive and reasonably mobile. We and she feel very lucky, because with multiple sclerosis you never know when things are going to deteriorate very rapidly.

Her husband was subsequently killed in an automobile accident, and she later lived with her son near Grants Pass, Oregon. Recently she has moved to a retirement community in Lacey, Washington. She has developed great skill in Chinese brush painting and now sells Chinese brush paintings. She has been to China studying at Huangzhou, perhaps the major art center in China. That has been her big hobby, and now she actually makes some money from it. Connie also inherited from my father and from our early family activities a great interest in travelling and seeing new places, although her illness in recent years has necessarily restricted that type of activity to a minimum.

My youngest sister, Peggie, is ten years younger than I. She was the one who was born shortly before my mother's death. Peggie did part of her high school work in Utah when my brother was living in Panguitch. She graduated from high school there and, being immersed in a largely Mormon community, became a devout Mormon herself. She went on to college at Utah State University in Logan, where she graduated with a degree in elementary education. She met her husband-to-be there, also a Mormon, who spent his career in electrical engineering employment. Peggie's principal endeavor has been raising a very happy family of five children. Two of the boys are mentally impaired, and the church has been a particular source of strength and support. The two are making their way in life working, and are productive citizens; the other three children all graduated from college. Peggie's husband has now retired, and the family lives in Mesa, Arizona. I see them often.

Family Relationships and Politics

Allen: I guess what is rather unusual is that every member of our family has complete confidence in and respect for one another. There is no problem in talking to any one of them about anything. Not all families can say that. My stepmother, who attended Wellesley and Pomona Colleges, was actually at one time my father's secretary at the Claremont Graduate University. She came from New York City and was born on Nantucket Island. She brought a degree of eastern influence to our family and had a liberalizing effect on us western "cowhands." She is still living in Claremont and is still reasonably active. She is an avid Democrat—as was my father—and she was active in the League of Women Voters and many community groups.

Scott: What about the politics of your brothers and sisters? You have already said something about the political views of your cattleman brother in New Mexico.

Allen: I would put my oldest sister in the same category as my father and stepmother. My younger sister, like many Mormons, tends to be somewhat more conservative. My brother, I am sure, is a political independent. I said before that he tended to be anti-environmentalist, but that's not quite the right word. On the contrary, he considers himself the ultimate environmentalist—one who loves the wilderness so much that he chooses to live there and make his career there, in harmony with the environment. He doesn't, however, have much patience with what he would call the "Hollywood environmentalists," whom he views as often totally unrealistic, totally ignorant about the back country, and fundamentally selfish and arrogant in their outlook. On foreign and domestic political policy, he's an independent—certainly not the ultra-conservative that many ranchers are. Quite naturally, he tends to be aghast at government bureaucracy, which he sees constantly in trying to deal with the Forest Service and Bureau of Land Management. I can understand that and tend to be sympathetic.

Chapter 2

1942-1946: Reed College and World War II

I did a lot of flying over Japan during that year. I flew over both Hiroshima and Nagasaki only weeks after the bombs were dropped, and they were sights I'll never forget.

Scott: When you graduated from high school, did you go straight into college?

Allen: Yes. I was too young to get into the army when I graduated from Claremont High School in 1942, with World War II already in progress. My father had already volunteered and gone back into the service as a "retread" from World War I. By 1941 he was already on his way overseas, and he ended up as classification officer for the Fifth Air Force in the Far East. His ship was kamikazied in Leyte Gulf, and he probably actually put in more real "combat" service than either my older brother or myself.

Choosing Reed College

Allen: Still too young for military service, I
started college. I had grown up around
Pomona College and knew the institution very
well. It was a small liberal arts college, but I did
not particularly want to go to college in my
own home town, particularly one where my
father had been a professor. I think it was a wise
decision on my part not to go there. So I ended
up going to Reed College in Portland.

Scott: Reed is a well-known liberal arts college with an excellent reputation. How did you
come to choose it?

Allen: Yes, with its liberal arts emphasis,
Reed is somewhat similar to Pomona College.
At least for that day and age, Reed had kind of
an avant-garde reputation. For example, it had
the reputation of being "Red" and so forth. But
I was looking for a small college in the West
that would be comparable to Pomona College.
Others considered were places like Occidental,
which was too close to home, or Whitman in
Walla Walla, Washington.

I was particularly interested in physics, and at
that time Reed had a strong association with
the University of Chicago, which was then the
premier physics university in the country. I
enjoyed my first year there at Reed. But by
1943, at the end of my first year there, I was old
enough to volunteer for military service.

Volunteering: Three Years
in the Service

Allen: When I volunteered, Reed and some
other colleges had Army people studying pre-
meteorology, to be trained to become meteorologists. I told my father I thought I would
join the pre-meteorology program. He said,
"You don't want to do that—you want to fly." I
said, "Who, me?" He said, "Yes, why don't you
become a cadet?" In contrast, some other parents essentially tried to talk their children out
of going into flying, where the casualty rate was
admittedly rather high—certainly higher than
among meteorologists. I took my father's
advice and applied to go into the aviation cadet
program of the U.S. Army Air Corps, rather
than going into the pre-meteorology program.
I was probably rather lucky I did this, because
as it turned out they trained too many meteorologists, and a lot of them ended up in the
infantry in Germany.

At the time, my father was stationed tempo-
rarily in Florida. I was down there for the summer, was inducted in Jacksonville, Florida, in
August 1943, and did initial basic training in
Keesler Field, Mississippi. In the fall they sent
me to Superior, Wisconsin, just as the harbor
froze; and the day the ice broke, they sent me
down to Texas for the next summer. I ended up
getting my commission as an airplane navigator
in November of 1944. I had a choice of bombardier training, pilot training, or navigation. I
chose navigation because of my early interest in
maps and geography, and am glad I did. It was a
lot of fun. In fact, I do not think I have ever
done anything in my life that I enjoyed as much
as aerial navigation, even though I certainly did
not think twice about staying in the Army at
the end of the war.

I eventually ended up in B-29 training and
served at various training locations all over the
country. That included Victorville, California,
which at that time was involved in bombardier
training, and I had to do some of that in con-

nection with radar bombing techniques. Then I went overseas in 1945, after our crew was formed at Pratt, Kansas. We took our airplane, a new B-29, and flew overseas. We were going to Okinawa. The Twentieth Air Force, the B-29 Air Force in the Far East, was based in the Marianas—Saipan and adjacent islands. They were then in the process of setting up another similar force—the Eighth Air Force—to be based in Okinawa.

General Jimmie Doolittle, who had been in Europe, came to be the first commander of the Eighth Air Force on Okinawa. We were the first of the B-29s to land in Okinawa, and I remember shaking hands with him then. This was just a few days after the atom bomb was dropped on Japan. Although combat was still going on in Okinawa, our particular group did not go into action over Japan during the war. Within a few weeks of my arrival, the Japanese surrendered. I was over there for about a year in all, most of it after the war had ended.

I did a lot of flying over Japan during that year. I flew over both Hiroshima and Nagasaki only weeks after the bombs were dropped, and they were sights I'll never forget. We did a lot of meteorological work over China, and I went down to the Philippines quite often. I was down there on Philippines Independence Day, July 4, 1946. We did typhoon reconnaissance work, where we flew into the middle of a typhoon and tried to figure out which way the winds were blowing and how hard. I also directed a program of radar photography of bridges and other potential targets along the 38th parallel in Korea, which was perhaps responsible for my being recalled very briefly to active duty in the Air Force in 1951 during

the Korean War. Although I enjoyed navigation, I had no interest in the military as a career, and so got out at the first opportunity, which was in October of 1946, after I had spent a little over three years total time in the service.

All in all, military service was a very valuable experience for me, both in terms of general maturation, and specifically in terms of whetting my interest in things that eventually took me into geology and geophysics as a profession. Like all military fliers, I had my fair share of close calls that came uncomfortably close to disaster—some of them resulting from my own navigational errors!—but luckily I survived in good shape and was, I think, a stronger person as a result. And not the least, military service permitted me to take advantage of the GI Bill to complete my collegiate education, which otherwise would have been financially difficult. What a different war from that later in Vietnam!

Return to Reed College

Allen: When I got out of the military, I returned to Reed College, where I found just about the same male fellow students as when I was there in 1942. We had all come back at about the same time. I continued my work in physics and got my degree there in physics in 1949. Reed did not have any geology program then. I had gotten interested in geology, partly because we had flown around in the Far East area where I had observed erupting volcanoes and things like that. Looking back, I wished many times that I again had that opportunity to fly almost wherever you wanted to, and with a camera.

Scott: Say a little more about your experience while at Reed College.

Allen: Reed had a very strong program in physics. I majored in physics, minored in history, and in the process really did get a broad education. By all odds the very best teacher I had at Reed was a history professor by the name of Dorothy Johansen.

At that time Reed College had a yearly prize essay award in the area of Pacific Northwest history. I spent a lot of time working on such a document and won the prize in 1949, and thus, my first scholarly publication was in history, not in geophysics or geology.[1] The essay was a study of a geographical misconception. When Lewis and Clark returned up the Columbia River following the winter encampment of 1905-1906 near its mouth, they noted the Willamette River coming in from the south with a tremendous volume of water. Subsequent mapmakers were aware of the water flow reported by Lewis and Clark, and being from the East could not imagine how the river could have that volume of water without its headwaters being in the Rocky Mountains. After all, the Columbia and Snake Rivers go way back into the Rocky Mountains. So their early maps show the Willamette River as originating somewhere far to the east in the Rocky Mountains.

I spent quite a bit of time at the Library of Congress one summer looking up old maps. The widely distributed map of the western U.S. showed the Willamette going on across Nevada and into Utah. Map makers not only couldn't imagine a river that big originating only in the coastal forest but also thought a big

body of water like Great Salt Lake must have an outlet. What could make more sense than to connect the two? Anyway, I had a lot of fun doing that essay, and as I say, it was my first publication.

Also as a result of my interest in history, I have been fascinated by local history. Here at Caltech, particularly in my retirement years, I have been leading a lot of field trips for people who support the institution financially. We have taken trips having a geologic interest to places such as Death Valley, Mt. St. Helens, Patagonia, and New Zealand. Our geologists here at Caltech lead or co-lead a number of these trips.

For the groups I have led, I always try to get in some of the local history, and that has been a lot of fun. For example for a trip to the San Juan Islands a few years ago, I had a chance to read up about the Pig War, which was a virtual war between the United States and Britain in that area. In Death Valley, it was the Manly Party, and down in South America we talked a lot about Charles Darwin and some of the things he did and saw there. In fact I have been to almost all the places in Chile where Darwin was. He was a truly remarkable observer. That is all a heritage from my interest in history that goes back to the work I did at Reed.

Geophysics: A Fortunate Recommendation

Allen: I worked one summer for the Naval Research Laboratory in Washington, D.C. My father was in Washington on an assignment for the Brookings Institution. At the end of the summer, I drove with my parents back to the West Coast. When we got to Madison, Wis-

---

1.   Allen, C.R., "The Myth of the Multnomah: The History of a Geographical Misconception," *Reed College Bulletin*. Vol. 27, p. 91-113, 1949.

consin, my stepmother became very ill, and we stopped over. Her family had some friends in Madison by the name of C.K. Leith. He was an eminent geologist who had become very wealthy in the iron ranges of Minnesota.

I got to talking with him, while we were waiting several days for my mother to get better, and expressed some of the frustration I had with physics, and the fact that I did not want to spend the rest of my life in a physics laboratory. He said, "Well, why don't you think about geophysics?" That was the first time I had even heard the word. In geophysics you essentially use physics to try to solve geological problems. Most geophysicists then were working for oil companies, using seismic methods and gravity methods and so forth to tell where there was oil.

I still thank God that we stopped in Madison, Wisconsin, that time so many years ago, where the old geologist urged me to think about geophysics. I honestly do not think I would have made a very good physicist. Although I passed all the math courses I ever took with good grades, clearly abstract thinking is not for me, and I do not think I would have been a top-notch physicist at all, and certainly not a mathematician. In some ways, I believe I think more like an engineer than a scientist. This is partly due to the fact that I'm not very good at abstract thinking, and partly due to my interest in practical kinds of things.

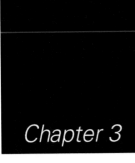

Chapter 3

Caltech: Graduate Work and Joining the Faculty

. . . Beno Gutenberg, Charlie Richter, and Hugo Benioff. They were three of the most eminent seismologists of their day, all there in adjacent offices in one building.

Thesis on the San Andreas Fault

Allen: Because geophysics sounded very attractive, when I applied for graduate work, I made inquiries as to what schools had geophysics departments and applied to several of them including the University of California at Los Angeles (UCLA), Caltech, and I think U.C. Berkeley. I came to Caltech essentially because the executive officer of the department wrote me a very nice letter. That man, incidentally, was Ian Campbell, who was later to become an eminent California State Geologist, and in that post, headed the Division of Mines and Geology. Caltech did not offer any scholarship money, but I had the GI Bill plus the California State bill for GIs. In his letter, Ian made the place sound so attractive that I came here. Had I gone to UCLA, I would probably have gone into studies of different types. Geophysics covers a lot of fields, and includes things like studies of the upper atmosphere, which UCLA was particularly strong in at the time.

Scott: Geophysics takes in all of planet Earth, from the outer reaches of its atmosphere down to its very center, doesn't it?

Allen: Yes, that's the way the word is usually interpreted. Sometimes we even get into rather inane arguments as to whether geophysics is a branch of geology, or whether geology is a branch of geophysics.

I came here to Caltech not knowing a great deal about the school. I knew that earthquakes were one thing they studied, but also at that time they had a fairly strong program in what we called applied geophysics, in things like finding oil and finding ore deposits. To make the transition into geophysics, during the summer of 1949 I studied at the University of Colorado summer program solely in geology. Then I started out here in geophysics, but gradually shifted more and more towards geology.

By the time I wrote my doctor's thesis, I was working almost entirely in geology. I particularly enjoyed field geology—mapping rocks in the field and trying to understand their origin and geologic history. My thesis supervisor was Dick Jahns, a remarkable guy, who was then on the faculty here at Caltech. He later went to Pennsylvania State University, and finally became dean of earth sciences at Stanford. It was a lot of fun to work with him. He was a very perceptive geologist and had a great sense of humor. I really enjoyed doing my thesis with him as advisor.

I received my doctorate in 1954, my major being in geology and my minor in geophysics. I did my thesis on a study of the San Andreas fault zone in the San Gorgonio Pass area between San Bernardino and Palm Springs.[2] Much of this was and still is a remote area on the south slopes of San Gorgonio Peak. In parts of this area, I even had to make my own topographic maps, using aerial photographs and photogrammetric equipment, before I could map the geology on the ground.

I enjoyed that field work a great deal. It was an area that I had picked out, and was structurally very complicated. While I was aware that the San Andreas fault was a major producer of earthquakes, my interest then was more in structural geology and the structural relations of rocks, than in earthquakes per se. One of the major geologic controversies of the time was whether or not the San Andreas fault had had very large cumulative displacements on it—perhaps hundreds of miles—and I was much more interested at the time in whether the distribution of rock units on the two sides of the fault supported that idea than I was in the problems of contemporary earthquakes along the fault.

Glacier Studies

Allen: As you know, graduate students are asked to take graduate assistantships, in which one serves as a research assistant to a professor. At one point I was assigned to Hugo Benioff, who had me trying to design a different kind of seismometer. I also worked with Charles Richter. So while I was at Caltech, I gradually

2. Allen, C.R., "The San Andreas Fault Zone in San Gorgonio Pass, Southern California," *Geological Society of America Bulletin.* Vol. 68, p. 315-350, 1957.

became associated with people active in earthquake work. I became very much interested in it, and that interest has persisted and intensified throughout my career. I also did a good deal of work in geomorphology and glaciology.

For several summers after I got my degree, I carried out glaciological studies, trying to understand the structure of glaciers. What is the physical process by which ice flows? Since it flows and fractures at the same time, I was trying to understand the origins of the crevasse patterns and that sort of thing. I spent two summers on Malaspina Glacier in Alaska,[3] and parts of nine summers working on the Blue Glacier on Mt. Olympus, in Washington State.[4] We also documented for the first time the existence of former Pleistocene glaciers in southern California—specifically on Mount San Gorgonio and San Jacinto Peak.[5]

Scott: So you were pretty active in glacier studies at that time?

Allen: Yes, but in fact I think my major time was spent in structural geology, and I got more and more interested in studying faults.

3. Allen, C.R., and Smith, G.I., "Seismic and Gravity Investigations on the Malaspina Glacier, Alaska," *American Geophysical Union Transactions*. Vol. 34, p. 755-760, 1953.

4. Allen, C.R., Kamb, W.B., Meier, M.F., and Sharp, R.P., "Structure of the Lower Blue Glacier, Washington," *Journal of Geology*. Vol. 68, p. 601-625, 1960.

5. Sharp, R.P., Allen, C.R., and Meier, F.M., "Pleistocene Glaciers on Southern California Mountains," *American Journal of Science*. Vol. 257, p. 81-94, 1959.

Scott: What got you into the study of glaciers?

Allen: I got into glacier studies primarily due to Bob Sharp, who was a very inspiring professor of geomorphology here at Caltech. He always made a point of getting graduate students involved in his summer programs, and he got me involved. He is still a very close friend. Bob had some of the first research grants in our geology division, from the Office of Naval Research, trying to understand glaciers. At the same time, I, of course, continued my interest in fault systems. I was also working fairly closely with Charles Richter on some studies of seismicity in California.

A Year Teaching at Minnesota

Allen: When I graduated in 1954, I decided that I wanted to go into academic research and teaching, and in those days there were many openings available. I decided, however, that since my roots were mostly in the West, I would like to stay west of the Mississippi River. So when I was offered a job at the University of Minnesota in Minneapolis, I looked it up on the map. Sure enough, Minneapolis was on the west side of the Mississippi and St. Paul was on the east side. Only after I arrived there did I realize that one small part of Minneapolis is east of the river, and the University of Minnesota is located there. Thus, my first teaching job was in fact east of the Mississippi.

I enjoyed teaching there. I enjoyed the students and found a much broader intellectual interest among them than is the case at Caltech. I remember teaching elementary geology to pre-nursing students, and it was a lot of fun. I don't think I have enjoyed teaching a course as much as that one, where I was trying to stimulate interest in a group of people from a wholly different field. John Peter Buwalda, the structural geologist at Caltech, died during the year I was at Minnesota, and in the search to replace him, I was asked to come back. So after only about a year, I went back to Caltech. I had nothing against Minnesota; it was just that the opportunities here at Caltech were so great, particularly in the things that interested me—such as faults and earthquakes.

Let me digress slightly and talk about a fascinating job I had in the long summer after I left Caltech and before I started at Minnesota. Shell had just struck oil near Ely, Nevada, and various oil companies had hurriedly leased properties throughout the Great Basin, even though geologists did not yet understand the geologic source of the oil at Ely. Union Oil Company of California (now UNOCAL) hired me for the summer to find out all I could about the desert mountains of westernmost Utah, which were largely unknown geologically at that time.

Union provided me with a jeep, a carryall, a small house trailer, thousands of aerial photographs, a paleontologist, and a cook. They told us to stay in the boondocks and come into town for groceries and report in by mail once every two weeks. It was an exciting experience, doing reconnaissance geology in a remote area about which little was known, and, believe me, the winch on our jeep got a thorough workout during that summer! And as a result of our efforts, Union dropped all of its leases in the area—wisely, it turned out. My paleontologist stayed on with the company and later rose to a high position in its exploration division.

Joining the Caltech Faculty

Allen: Anyway, I came back to Caltech in late 1955, this time as a member of the faculty. When I had been a graduate student, I had spent quite a bit of time at the Seismological Laboratory, which was then in a separate group of buildings over on San Rafael Avenue on the west side of the Arroyo Seco. So when I came back and was on the faculty, I continued to spend a lot of time over there. It was very interesting because the three principal members of the group there were Beno Gutenberg, Charlie Richter, and Hugo Benioff. They were three of the most eminent seismologists of their day, all there in adjacent offices in one building.

Seismological Laboratory: Gutenberg, Benioff, and Richter

Scott: Say a little more about those three.

Allen: Each one was very distinctive. Beno Gutenberg was a gentleman scholar of the first order—very friendly, but very formal in the way he did things. He was the most organized person I have ever known. He would sit at his desk and write down the things he was doing on a pad of paper. Every note that he made was on a numbered sheet, which he carefully kept. Box after box of those notes are still on file in our building—essentially everything he ever wrote down. Even when solving equations, everything was written down and kept. He was an amazingly productive person and, in his day, was probably the world's most eminent seismologist.

Hugo Benioff started out being an astronomer, but did not like working nights, so he became a seismologist. He was a true genius in designing instruments. His main contributions are in various types of seismological instruments that he designed and built, working together with some fine mechanics and machinists at the laboratory. He was also very interested in tectonic processes, and I'll come back in a moment to a specific interaction I had with him in this area.

I probably knew Charlie Richter as well as did any other faculty member now here at Caltech. He and I co-authored several papers.[6,7] He was a brilliant person but also a very troubled person. He did not mix easily with other people. He was very protective of what he did and took great issue if anyone said anything that he considered an insult to his science. He had explosive emotional outbursts that were very difficult to deal with. Virtually all the students at the lab had at one time or another suffered under his temper tantrums, which in many cases were not at all logical. But he also had a great sense of humor. One of his books, *Elementary Seismology*, is sprinkled throughout with footnotes that represent humorous episodes.[8]

When Charlie got the galley proofs back for *Elementary Seismology* from the printer, I volunteered to read it out loud to him. So day after day, I sat reading that book to him from cover to cover. I learned a lot about the book, and I also learned a lot more about Charlie Richter. I owe a lot to Charlie, and I was the one who wrote the obituary for him that appeared in the *Seismological Society of America Bulletin* in 1987.[9] I am rather proud of this piece, because he was a hard man to characterize. It was a very difficult writing job, because he was a troubled person and not everything said could be totally complimentary, but I think it came out as a rather nice statement.

In the public eye, because of the Richter Scale, he is probably the most famous seismologist in the world. I think he certainly deserves major credit for developing the original Richter Scale, admittedly under Gutenberg's tutelage. That was an important contribution, but not nearly as important as the public would seem to think. Between Richter and Gutenberg, there is no question that the latter made the greater scientific contribution. I do not say this to belittle Charles, but to point out that he stands unduly high in public opinion because the Richter Scale is so well known. But I consider *Elementary Seismology* to be his greatest contribution to science.

An Interesting Interaction with Hugo Benioff

Allen: At one point, Hugo Benioff came up with a hypothesis about the rotation of the Pacific Ocean basin. Benioff was a brilliant seismologist and a very imaginative guy with all sorts of ideas, about half of which turned out to be dead wrong, but the other half proved bril-

6. Richter, C.F., Allen, C.R., and Nordquist, J.M., "The Desert Hot Springs Earthquakes and their Tectonic Environment," *Seismological Society of America Bulletin*. Vol. 48, p. 315-337, 1958.

7. Allen, C.R., St. Amand, P., Richter, C.F., and Nordquist, J.M., "Relationship between Seismicity and Geologic Structure in the Southern California Region," *Seismological Society of America Bulletin*. Vol. 55, p. 753-797, 1965.

8. Richter, C.F., Elementary Seismology, W.H. Freeman and Co., San Francisco, California. 768 pages, 1958.

9. Allen, C.R., "Charles Richter: A Personal Tribute," *Seismological Society of America Bulletin*. Vol. 77, p. 2234-2237, 1987.

liant. He developed a hypothesis that the Pacific Ocean basin was rotating with respect to the circum-Pacific regions around it. Here in California we have a right-handed fault, and there are right-handed faults in parts of Alaska, and parts of New Zealand. (I should point out that a right-handed or right-lateral fault is one on which, when you face it, the far side has moved horizontally to your right.) Because of all these right-handed faults around the edge of the Pacific Basin, Benioff got the idea that perhaps the entire basin was rotating in a counterclockwise fashion relative to the surrounding continental regions. This was before the concept of plate tectonics had been developed, so the idea of any very large piece of the earth's surface being a rigid plate moving with respect to the country around it was rather unique.

In the meantime, I had gotten involved in working down in Chile, where there was a suspicion of a major fault zone similar to the San Andreas. Frank Press, who had then joined the Caltech Seismological Laboratory faculty—and who later became the President's science advisor and still later president of the National Academy of Sciences—obtained some funds to support my field work there. I recall that in Chile I came down with a very severe case of infectious hepatitis and left only shortly before the 1960 earthquake. For a geologist or seismologist that was unfortunate, as we like to be on the spot during a big earthquake, and I just missed the big Chilean earthquake in 1960. It was the world's largest earthquake of the 20th century, a magnitude 9.5.

Anyway, I was working down in Chile with Pierre St. Amand, who had been a fellow graduate student at Caltech and was then on a USAID assignment in Chile. We found strike-slip faults that had not previously been mapped, and they were right-handed faults just like those here in California.[10] I told Benioff about this, and he said, "This really fits the Pacific rotation idea well." "But," he also said, "there are some large areas over in the Far East where we do not have much information." He asked if I could find out something about that. In reading the literature, I became aware of a major strike-slip fault parallel to the east coast of Taiwan. Also in the Philippines, I learned that in the early part of the century, Bailey Willis, an eminent Stanford geologist, had suggested a big strike-slip fault—the Philippine fault—but without getting any idea of what its sense of displacement was.

In 1952, Benioff found the money for me to go to the Philippines in hopes that I would find right-handed faults there to support the idea of a rotating Pacific Basin. I mapped that fault at some length and am proud of the work I did there. I spent a lot of time in Leyte, where the fault was nicely exposed. In those days, it was geologic exploration in a very real sense.

These were not, however, the right-handed faults that Benioff had hoped I would find, because I discovered that the faults parallel to the Pacific's rim in both the Philippines and Taiwan were left-handed.[11] The left-handed displacement was very clear, mostly from the

10. Allen, C.R.,"Transcurrent Faults in Continental Areas," *Royal Society of London Philosophical Transactions.* A, Vol. 258, p. 82-89, 1965.

11. Allen, C.R., "Circum-Pacific Faulting in the Philippines-Taiwan Region," *Journal of Geophysical Research.* Vol. 67, p. 4795-4812, 1962.

evidence of offset stream channels, as well as some other evidence. Because of this evidence, Benioff threw away his theory. Also, there were other problems with it. The Pacific Basin is not really a circular plate—there were too many sharp corners in the boundary. So that was one of Benioff's many ideas that did not jell, and I guess I contributed to its demise. It did, however, represent some of the kinds of ideas that later came forth in the concept of plate tectonics.

Benioff had other important influences that I should acknowledge. My involvement with

earthquake consulting—rather than studying earthquakes solely as a subject of academic research—came about early, thanks mainly to Hugo Benioff. To this day I do a fair amount of consulting work, with emphasis on seismic hazard assessment. Hugo was responsible for my appointment in 1963 to the State Department of Water Resources' Consulting Board for Earthquake Analysis, where I first became associated with George Housner. We'll talk more about that later [see Chapter 6, Consulting on Major Dams and Water Projects].

Chapter 4

Field Studies of Faults and the Geology of Earthquakes

The biggest problem is that you are working from a basically planar exposure to try and figure out what relationships exist at depth.

Allen: I have always enjoyed the field aspect of geology. I particularly like the opportunity to work in remote parts of the world and to get out into the boondocks—quite aside from the geologic interest. I have found it fascinating to be in remote areas of the world and try to learn a little more about their cultures. For example, I have been in Tibet several times and have found it a fascinating place, not only for its geology, but also for its history, religion, architecture, politics, and so forth.

Scott: So when you go to those places, you not only study the geology and geophysics, but also try to get acquainted with many aspects of the people's lives?

Allen: Yes. I have had opportunities to go to remote places that few other people have had. In 1979, for example, I led the first group of foreign scientists that was ever allowed into Tibet, at least since the turn of the century.[12] I have been back several times subsequently, and I'll talk in a few minutes about a specific field study I did there in 1986.

Virtually all of these studies abroad have been carried out cooperatively with foreign scientists, and you'll see their names among the authors of the various resulting papers. Joint financial support has also been typical, with, for example, the National Science Foundation or the U.S. Geological Survey supporting American participation, and local national organizations supporting participation by foreign scientists. This has been true, for example, in my 11 trips to China and has worked out rather nicely.

We tried to arrange it so the time the American participants spent in China would be balanced by the amount of time the Chinese had over here. The big advantage was that when they were here, we covered their expenses, and when we were there, they covered ours. That last point was terribly important. In China, tourists and visitors pay far higher rates than do Chinese government institutions. By working through their government institutions and at their much lower rates, we scaled down our

expenses. Working independently, we could never have done what we did. They could not believe that the rates we paid for them here in Pasadena, such as motel charges, were the same as anyone else would pay. In China, government people would have to pay only maybe one-eighth of what a tourist would pay.

Field Geology and Geologic Mapping

Scott: At this point, would you say something about what field geologists actually do? For the benefit of future readers, describe what you actually did when you went out in the boondocks.

Allen: Field geology represents an attempt to understand the relationship and history of various rock units. If you can look at a photograph and learn enough to understand that, fine, you do not have to go out in the field. But geological relationships are usually so complicated that one typically has to go out in the field and try to understand how the various rocks are geometrically related and what the age relationships are. That is much easier said than done.

The problem with most introductory students—I have taught introductory geology here for many years—is that they want to go out in the field, walk around the area, figure it out, and then come back and make a geologic map. Well, if you could do it that easily you would probably not have to send out a trained geologist. Instead, you figure things out only by making the map and in the process trying to understand the relationships. If you find some relationships that do not seem to be compatible, you go back out and look it over again,

12. Bally, A.W., Allen, C.R., Geyer, G.R., Hamilton, R.B., Hopson, C.A., Molnar, P., Oliver, J.E., Opdyke, J.E., Plafker, G., and Wu, F.T., *Notes on the Geology of Tibet and Adjacent Areas—Report of the American Plate Tectonics Delegation to the People's Republic of China.* U.S. Geological Survey Open-File Report 80-501, 100 p., 1980.

maybe try to collect more fossils to demonstrate some age relationships, or collect samples for radiometric dating where that is critical.

In the case of studying active faults, which is only one small branch of geology, one tries to identify those features that will reveal whether or not a fault is present and what its degree of activity is. Is the fault currently active, what is its history, how recently have there been displacements, and what is the likelihood of future movements? Again, this is a lot easier said than done.

Scott: When you are out in the field poking around, do you mostly look for what you find on the surface? Do you look especially for cuts or other places of exposure? In a lot of the wilderness country, of course, you aren't likely to find nice neat road cuts where you might want them.

Allen: You are usually looking in areas of some relief, and there you have cuts in streams and so forth. The biggest problem is that you are working from a basically planar exposure to try and figure out what relationships exist at depth. Sometimes you are more successful than at other times. A lot depends on the degree of vegetative cover. In New Zealand, for example, with all the bush, it is very difficult to do geologic mapping. In some areas—such as in the Philippines—we have found ourselves clawing our way through the jungle. It can be much more difficult than you might imagine. Also, of course, to understand complicated local situations, geologists use many methods other than surface mapping, such as digging trenches, drilling boreholes, and a variety of geophysical techniques.

What a lot of people do not understand, however, is that the geologic map itself is not the objective. The map is a tool by which you

develop an understanding of the relationships. A physicist or biologist studying a problem may use a notebook to record the data. What is in the notebook is terribly critical, but the notebook itself is not the objective. It is the tool or technique that leads you to draw an important conclusion, and it represents the raw observational data from which others might judge whether or not they agree with your conclusion.

Scott: I guess the map is roughly analogous to the notebook—a method for recording and organizing the data?

Allen: Yes. We like to have students take at least an introductory course in field geology, even if they are to be geochemists or geophysicists. They need to see what the real world looks like. It is amazing how many of them later say something like, "The most valuable course I ever took at Caltech was that introductory field geology course that you bastards made me take." They develop a feel for how complicated things can be. They develop a grasp of the fact that Mother Nature has already done the experiment, and the field geologist is just trying to understand what happened. There are thousands of variables, and it is a very different problem from those that other scientists are used to attacking.

Scott: That is not like experiments conducted in a physics or chemistry laboratory, where the variables are typically very strictly controlled.

Allen: That's right, it is not like the laboratory where you set up the number of variables you want to investigate. Trying to understand Mother Nature's experiment and what she did to result in what you find in the field today is very challenging. It is not surprising that controversies and differences of opinion develop.

Scott: And different interpretations can each look pretty persuasive, each in its own way.

Allen: Yes. Different geologists have different attitudes toward field geology. I happen to enjoy field geology, and much of my career has involved looking at faults in the field. That is why I went to the Philippines and Sumatra, for example, to try to find field evidence of the degree of fault activity. It can be difficult, but also rewarding and fun.

Studying Major Active Faults

Allen: As a result of studying the fault in Chile, the big fault in Taiwan, the fault in the Philippines, and visiting New Zealand where major early work on the Alpine fault system was done by local geologists, I devoted more and more of my attention to studying major active faults. I was trying to better understand their relationship to earthquakes. The rest of my career has mostly been devoted to the geology of earthquakes, trying to understand major faults, how major earthquakes are generated, and in more recent years, to understand how this knowledge can be used in assessing and dealing with seismic hazards.

So for a number of years, I took advantage of every opportunity I could to visit and study areas where there were major faults of suspected strike-slip displacement, similar to the San Andreas. I found funds to get to Turkey on three or four different occasions, and spent a fair amount of time on the North Anatolian fault of that country.[13] Working together with Turkish geologists, we discovered a lot of interesting things about the North Anatolian fault, including a number of seismic gaps—segments of the fault that had not broken during the most recent series of earthquakes along the fault. These were considered particularly likely areas for earthquakes in the near future, and some of these gaps have, in fact, ruptured since the time of our work there. Later I had a chance to visit the great Sumatran fault in Indonesia, another similar feature.[14]

In more recent years, I have worked a lot in China and found some faults there that are similar to, but much more active than, the San Andreas fault. Thus, they offer some opportunities for studies that we simply cannot carry out on the San Andreas because of the lower frequency of earthquakes here, and also because there are longer records of historic earthquakes on the Chinese faults, where big earthquakes have repeated historically on the same segment of the fault.[15] With few exceptions, this is not true anywhere here in California. We have had big historic earthquakes on

13.   Allen, C.R., "Comparisons Between the North Anatolian Fault of Turkey and the San Andreas Fault of California," *Progress in Earthquake Prediction Research*. Vol. 2. Braunschweig/Wiesbaden, Friedrich Vieweg & Sohn. 578 pages, 1982.

14.   Untung, M., Buyung, M., Kertapati, E., and Allen, C.R., "Rupture Along the Great Sumatran Fault Zone, Indonesia, During the Earthquakes of 1926 and 1943," *Seismological Society of America Bulletin*. Vol. 75, p. 313-317, 1985.

15.   Allen, C.R., Luo, Z., Qian, H., Wen, Z., Zhou, H., and Huang, W., "Field Study of a Highly Active Fault Zone: the Xianshuihe Fault of Southwestern China," *Geological Society of America Bulletin*. Vol. 103, p. 1178-1199, 1991.

the San Andreas fault, but have seldom had them repeat in the same place.

Examples of Field Geology: Sumatra and the Philippines

Allen: The great Sumatran fault, which extends for more than 1000 miles from one end of the island to the other, had long been thought to be a right-handed strike-slip fault. There had been no earthquakes on it, however, on which right-lateral movement had been observed, and no geological evidence in the way of offset stream channels or offset rock units had been discovered. The fault was thought to be right-handed mainly because of the regional plate tectonic relationships, not because of evidence found along the fault itself.

I went to Indonesia only after being sure we could get aerial photographs. In many places you can see from photographs exactly where the fault trace is, whereas on the ground and in the jungle, it can be difficult or nearly impossible if you do not know where to look.

Scott: Aerial photography is very useful in geologic field work, isn't it?

Allen: Aerial photographs are terribly valuable in the study of faults and many other geologic features. There was this one place in central Sumatra where the most recent trace of the fault appeared to go through a little village. So, with my Indonesian colleagues, we visited the village. We knew that in around 1946 there had been a large earthquake in the general vicinity. It turned out that the villagers did not speak the language of my Indonesian colleagues. Finally, we found a man who spoke

both the local language and Indonesian, and were able to communicate through him.

First, I got to within ten feet or so of the place where the fault went through the village as seen on our air photos. Then they found this old man who came out to where we were. I asked, "Have you ever felt an earthquake?" He got very animated and said, "Oh, yes, yes!" Since we knew that there had been a big earthquake there in 1946, I asked, "Do you remember the 1946 earthquake?" "Oh, yes, yes, that occurred on a Friday!" (This is a Moslem area, as is most of Indonesia, and they seem to remember things by the days of the week.) I asked, "What happened?" He said, "Oh, the ground shook like hell, and the houses fell down." I asked, "Were there any cracks in the ground?" "Oh, yes, yes, right through here." I tried to be careful then and asked, "Did one side go up and the other side go down?" He said, "Neither—the ground went like this," indicating right-handed horizontal movement with hand motions. When I asked how he knew it moved that way, he had a good explanation—some chicken coops had been split apart and so forth. Subsequently, we also found some boundaries of roads that had been offset in 1946 and were still preserved.

Scott: So the old man gave you a pretty accurate report?

Allen: Yes. I am describing this to illustrate why it can be a lot of fun doing field geology and trying to get information on historic earthquakes. This particular man also told us that the same thing had happened in 1926. Well, we looked back, and indeed were able to find that Gutenberg and Richter had seismologically recorded a big earthquake in 1926, and estimated its location, which was not right there where we were. I think their location was simply wrong. It had to have happened where we were, and subsequent examination of Gutenberg's original notes of the 1926 earthquake, stored here in Pasadena, allowed a revised location.

We have also done that in Turkey and, to some extent, in the Philippines. It makes field geology and earthquake investigations a lot of fun. Incidentally, I don't mean to imply that a major part of our field work is in obtaining anecdotal reports from people; much more effort is spent in documenting fault locations, geologic histories of recent displacements—for example, by excavating trenches—slip-rate determinations, and so forth.

There was a big earthquake, magnitude 7.0, in the Philippines while I happened to be in Taiwan in 1973. After that earthquake, I heard some stories of a rail line having been displaced on the Tayabas Isthmus, about 100 miles southeast of Manila. Jack Oliver, now a professor emeritus at Cornell, and I went down, and with some Philippine friends found where the offset had crossed the highway and railroad. It had continued on south into the jungle, but we did not know where it had come out at the south coast. So we chartered a little boat. We went along the coast for an hour and a half, and then said, "Well, the fault should have come out somewhere around here," where there was a small village in the coconut groves.

For a time we got stuck on the reef trying to get into the village, but finally made it and found that the school teacher spoke English. We asked if they remembered the recent earthquake. "Oh, yes." "Were there any places where the ground was fissured?" "Oh yes, right over here." The spot where the fault had come through was only a hundred yards away. You could also tell it from the offset of the lines of coconut trees. So after an hour and a half of more or less blindly going south in the boat, we had the good luck to stop right at the place we should have.

You will recall my saying that the Philippine fault was a strike-slip fault and left-handed. Other people thought I was wrong and were saying it was not a strike-slip fault. Some German geologists were claiming that it was strike-slip, but right-handed. This was the first earthquake we had had on the fault in many years, and thank God it was left-handed, and we could prove it. That made me feel a little better. Also, in 1990 there was a much larger earthquake in Luzon north of Manila, a magnitude 7.8, and it was again satisfying to find that the displacement on the Philippine fault was left-handed, and that the break was along the exact line that I had discovered and mapped for the first time 28 years earlier as part of Benioff's "expedition."

Field Work in Tibet

Allen: One of the reasons that I went to eastern Tibet in 1986 was that we had identified on satellite images a fault several hundred miles long that looked remarkably similar to the San Andreas. Chinese geologists had earlier carried out field studies of a major earthquake that occurred on this fault in 1973 of magnitude 7.6, and I was curious as to whether earlier historic earthquakes had occurred on the same fault, known locally as the Xianshuihe fault, and how their features of displacement might be preserved. The area was quite remote, and I arranged a cooperative study with Chinese geologists from Chengdu, who fortunately provided logistical support. The high altitude and sparse vegetation led to remarkable preservation of surficial features, and we were surprised to be able to identify in 1986 open fissures resulting from not only the 1973 earthquake, but also from earlier displacements in 1923 and 1894—and even an offset berm from an earthquake known to have occurred in the region in 1816.

Among other things that had attracted me to this fault was a photograph taken in 1930 by an eminent Swiss geologist, Albert Heim, who had been in the area on a mountain-climbing expedition (nearby Gongga Shan is almost 25,000 feet high!). A local missionary had shown Heim a series of en-echelon cracks in the ground that were said to have been associated with a major earthquake there in 1923, and Heim published a photograph of this rupture in his report on the expedition. With some effort (and climbing!), we were able in 1986 to locate the exact spot from which Heim had taken his photograph, and the same fissures—now somewhat degraded—were still visible in 1986![16]

Buddhist lamas from local lamaseries were also very helpful in recounting stories of various earthquakes and ground displacements along the fault. Talking with them was fascinating. Many of the lamaseries had been tragically decimated during the Chinese cultural revolution in the 1960s. But at least by the time I was there in 1986, many lamas were still present, and we were told that at least one of the lamaseries was being rebuilt with help from Beijing. I can testify that it was being rebuilt, although I can't verify the source of the funds. It is interesting that in 1986, many of the Tibetan children were wearing buttons bearing a picture of the Dali Lama, although when I was in the same area several years later, following the Tiananmen Square episode in Beijing, I saw not a single such button. Times had changed!

Well, one of the important results of this field study was that we were able to show that historic earthquakes had repeated faithfully in almost every detail (that is, rupture location, rupture length, amount of displacement, etc.) along some segments of the Xianshuihe fault. I mentioned earlier that this has seldom been documented in California, because of lower rates of fault activity here as well as a shorter historic record. It's an important and controversial issue—related to that of the so-called characteristic earthquake—that is important in seismic hazard assessment.[17]

Scott: Is the available historical record in Tibet significantly longer than here?

Allen: It is in this particular part of Tibet, eastern Tibet. Actually, we were in westernmost Sichuan Province, but in an area on the Tibetan Plateau with a Tibetan population. The record there goes back into the 1700s. That is, of course, very short compared with what is found in the rest of China. But it is a

16. Allen, C.R., Luo, Z., Qian, H., Wen, Z., Zhou, H., and Huang, W., "Field Study of a Highly Active Fault Zone: the Xianshuihe Fault of Southwestern China," *Geological Society of America Bulletin*. Vol. 103, p. 1178-1199, 1991.

17. Yeats, R.S., Sieh, K., and Allen, C.R., *The Geology of Earthquakes*, Chapter 13. Oxford University Press, New York. 568 pages, 1997.

better record than we have in this country, at least here on the Pacific coast.

In all these endeavors, I teamed up with local geologists in the country I visited, and found these all very exciting experiences. I not only enjoyed the geology, but also the culture, the cuisine, the politics, and the history.

Scott: Regarding your enjoyment of the history, politics and culture, how did you go about this? Did you just keep your eyes open and observe what you saw and heard and were given to eat, or did you perhaps do some advance reading on the country visited?

Allen: Obviously you have to be careful. You do not want to get diverted and still have Caltech paying for your time. But you do a lot of talking to people. We have had a lot of fun talking to local residents about earthquakes in the recent historic past. The experience in Sumatra that I mentioned earlier is typical.

San Andreas Fault

Allen: As a result of my Ph.D. thesis work, I became particularly intrigued with the San Andreas fault. I then became aware that there were similar faults in other parts of the world—several examples of which I have just told you about. It is interesting that at one time, strike-slip faulting was thought to be almost unique to the San Andreas fault, although a similar feature had been discovered in New Zealand at about the time I was in graduate school at Caltech. From reading the literature, looking at maps and so forth, I became convinced that some of the features resembling the San Andreas were also very important in other places. This is what led me to take advantage of

the opportunity to go to the Philippines in connection with the basin-rotation controversy that Benioff had brought up.

Scott: Say a little more about strike-slip faulting, once considered almost unique to the San Andreas.

Allen: The San Andreas fault's strike-slip character, as well as its length, was thought to set it apart from other faults. The Russian tectonics people, on the other hand, even denied that any such faults existed, and talked entirely about vertical tectonics. Also, another controversy came up at that time. Everyone knew that the San Andreas had moved horizontally some 15 to 20 feet in the 1906 earthquake, but very little was known about its earlier history or what its total horizontal displacement might have been over the past few millions of years.

About 35 miles northeast of Los Angeles, on the north side of the San Gabriel Mountains and just south of the San Andreas fault, is an area of very scenic and distinctive tilted rocks known as the Devil's Punchbowl. Back in 1928, an eminent USGS geologist, Levi Noble, reported what he thought to be similar rocks in the Cajon Pass area on the opposite side of the fault that were separated by 25 miles. That would mean a total of 25 miles of right-handed horizontal displacement since the time those rocks had been laid down. Back when he said that, he was scoffed at—"That's absolutely ridiculous." Most geologists simply did not understand how the movement could be that large. No one could deny the 1906 offset up to the north being horizontal, but it was considered unthinkable that the movement in the

Cajon Pass area (or elsewhere along the fault) totaled some 25 miles.

Somewhat later, in the early 1950s, however, two eminent petroleum geologists, Mason Hill and Tom Dibblee, proposed that the total displacement on the San Andreas fault was some 150 miles, and this caused even more controversy. Similarly about this time, the New Zealanders proposed that there had been several hundred miles of displacement on their big fault, the Alpine fault.

Those controversies were among the intriguing things that were going on at about that time, as I mentioned earlier in connection with my Ph.D. thesis work in San Gorgonio Pass. Nowadays, of course, whereas Noble was criticized in 1928 for postulating a displacement of as much as 25 miles, his estimate is now considered ridiculously low—it's much more than that. The geologists advocating the existence of large displacements have largely turned out to be right. Now it all fits in with ideas about plate tectonics and large motions of tectonic plates.

Seismic Hazard Evaluation

Allen: As time went by, I became aware that the kind of work I was doing was very relevant to seismic hazard evaluation, which was critical for land-use planning and the design of earthquake-resistant structures. I was looking at active faults—that is, those now capable of producing earthquakes. I wanted to know how you could say a fault was active or not. We have found out that there are all degrees of fault activity, and any kind of simple distinction is arbitrary. So, one problem in hazard evaluation is to quantify the degree of a fault's activity. You cannot just say that a fault is safe, or unsafe. You need to say something like this: "Here are the chances that the fault might break—do you want to take those chances or don't you?" That is the probabilistic approach that is now being used a great deal—a subject I want to return to later.

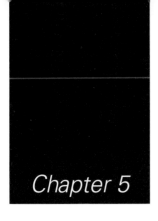

Chapter 5

Colleagues and Work at Caltech

I'll never forget trudging up the Cañon de Dolores in the intense summer heat, leading our trusty packhorse.

Caltech Colleagues

Scott: Would you say something about some of your later colleagues at Caltech and the work you have done with them?

Dick Jahns

Allen: Although Dick Jahns left Caltech in 1960, he was my Ph.D. thesis advisor and played an important role in my career at Caltech, not only when I was a graduate student, but also later as a young faculty member. He is largely responsible for whetting my appetite for, and honing my skills in, field geology. To him, a good geologic map was a real work of art, and he was also a real hound on clear, concise writing. Finally, he was the instigator of almost daily afternoon touch-football games that drew geology students and faculty members together and helped keep morale at a high level.

Bob Sharp and Leon Silver

Allen: I have already mentioned Bob Sharp, who played a very important part in my career and, in particular, got me involved in glacial work. He was sort of a father figure for many years.

Leon T. Silver is another colleague who has been important to me. He is a geologist and petrologist. We had been students here together and then joined the faculty at the same time. We have been close friends and have worked together on a number of projects. One of my first non-San Andreas fault studies was really a pioneering study of a major fault that we first recognized in Baja California, about 100 miles south of Ensenada. He and I spent two or three summers working on that fault system, and I'll never forget trudging up the Cañon de Dolores in the intense summer heat, leading our trusty packhorse. His expertise was in rock types, and identification of rock types was important in trying to understand the displacement along the faults. Which rocks were juxtaposed against which other rocks, and how far had they moved to get there? He and I published that work together, along with a third colleague.[18]

Lee and I have also taught field geology together. Only a short time ago, we ran a trip together for our Associates—supporters of Caltech—to visit the mining districts of central Colorado. I have learned a lot from Lee, and the association has been enjoyable.

18. Allen, C.R., Silver, L.T., and Stehli, F.G., "Agua Blanca Fault—A Major Transverse Structure of Northern Baja California, Mexico," *Geological Society of America Bulletin*. Vol. 71, p. 457-482, 1960.

Kerry Sieh

Allen: I am largely responsible for Kerry Sieh being at Caltech. Sieh is now generally recognized as the father of paleoseismology. He did his Ph.D. thesis work at Stanford—really seminal work digging trenches across the San Andreas fault near Wrightwood. Sieh had earlier been an undergraduate student at the University of California at Riverside.

Scott: When Kerry Sieh read your oral history in draft form, he observed that you played a pivotal role in his professional development. He indicated that except for your advice at a crucial time, he would probably not even be in the field of earthquake geology today.

Allen: I'm very grateful for Kerry's nice words. What happened was that, in Kerry's initial graduate work at Stanford, he was unable to find a professor interested in sponsoring the type of fault studies in which he was interested, and he contemplated leaving school altogether. Since I had known him earlier and was familiar with his talents and interests, he came down to Caltech to seek my advice. I encouraged him to stay at Stanford, and, in particular, to try to work with Dick Jahns, who, as I mentioned earlier, had been my Ph.D. thesis advisor at Caltech and was then the dean of the School of Earth Sciences at Stanford. Kerry had evidently felt deans were unapproachable, but at my urging, he got together with Dick and found the same inspirational and compatible person that I had. He then successfully completed his degree and is now perhaps the leading figure in the world in paleoseismology. So I'll take credit for giving a little encouragement and doing a little pushing, but Dick Jahns can be given credit for really "turning Kerry on."

Kerry and I have worked together on a number of projects, including one of the major faults in Yunnan Province, China.[19] Kerry joined the Caltech staff in 1977. Also, he, more than anyone else at Caltech, represents the filling of the vacancy left when I retired. He is perhaps more of a pure geologist than I am. I am really split between geology and seismology. Kerry is also now deeply involved in a lot of consulting on some of the same kinds of things I have been involved in, and his work is very important in seismic hazard assessments.

Hiroo Kanamori

Allen: Hiroo Kanamori is the former director of our Caltech Seismological Laboratory and is a scientist from whom I have learned a great deal and for whom I have utterly profound respect. He follows in the tradition of former world-renowned directors: Beno Gutenberg, Frank Press, and Don Anderson. Hiroo is a broadly trained seismologist, born and educated in Japan, who came to Caltech first as a research fellow in 1965 and then as a professor in 1972. I regard him as the outstanding seismologist in the world today. His physical insights and his imagination are simply fantastic. Although he and I have been co-authors on only a couple of papers, the most

significant of which involved the mechanics of earthquakes,[20] he has been a constant source of advice, wisdom, and new ideas.

Cohesive Faculty

Allen: The five men I have just mentioned have perhaps been the most important Caltech colleagues from my personal point of view. But the faculty of our Division of Geological and Planetary Sciences has been remarkably cohesive over the years, and I have had the opportunity to work with many of its members. Among present or former Caltech faculty members with whom I have authored scientific papers, in addition to those just mentioned, are Don Anderson, Jim Brune, Don Helmberger, George Housner, Bill Iwan, Paul Jennings, Barclay Kamb, Joe Kirschvink, Leon Knopoff, Frank Press, Charlie Richter, and Stewart Smith. I wish I could add the names of all the graduate students that I've also had the opportunity of jointly publishing with.

Scott: You speak of a cohesive faculty. I take it you have not had the kinds of feuds and infighting that many faculties sometimes experience?

Allen: We have had a few individual feuds, but not the kind where the division has been split asunder, as has unfortunately happened at some universities. When you have very intense and highly motivated people, some friction and disagreements are inevitable. But our division has, over the years, enjoyed remarkably forward-looking and unselfish leadership, starting

19. Allen, C.R., Gillespie, A.R., Han, Y., Sieh, K.E., Zhang, B., and Zhu, C., "Red River and Associated Faults, Yunnan Province, China: Quaternary Geology, Slip Rates, and Seismic Hazard," *Geological Society of America Bulletin*. Vol. 95, p. 686-700, 1984.

20. Kanamori, H., and Allen, C.R., "Earthquake Repeat Time and Average Stress Drop," *American Geophysical Union Geophysical Monograph 37*. p. 227-235, 1986.

with Bob Sharp, who was chairman when I first came on the faculty.

Similarly, during my tenure here, Caltech itself has enjoyed effective leadership in its presidents and provosts, and the institute represents a truly unique intellectual environment that many of my colleagues in other universities envy. Caltech's small size certainly helps to maintain this atmosphere, but, above all, it requires strong, enlightened, and unselfish leadership. I feel very fortunate to have been here during this period.

Chapter 6

Consulting on Major Dams and Water Projects

The designers wanted advice on whether the faults should be considered active, what kinds of earthquakes they might produce, and how often such earthquakes might happen.

Allen: I think my first consulting was with the California Department of Water Resources. Subsequently, I've been involved with any number of projects around the world, most of them involving big dams. I tended to stay out of the nuclear plant controversies because they got so emotional that the science tended to get lost. Also, since big money was involved, the proponents and opponents tended to develop opposing teams of experts. Team members on one side might start out respecting members of the other team, although considering them perhaps misguided. Eventually, however, after years of fighting, it could begin to get more personal, and there was a tendency not only to consider the opposing team wrong, but to rate them as a bunch of unethical bastards. "Team spirit" may have its place in some kinds of conflicts, but, in my opinion, it is not conducive to the resolution of scientific and technical issues.

Scott: You mean that after a few years of arguing over the technical issues, one side would develop a degree of downright antipathy for those on the other side?

Allen: Yes, and seeing that happening, I did not want to get involved. I was also involved in one case as an expert witness in court, and decided I did not want to get involved in any of those again. Hugo Benioff got me into that case, which was on a groundwater issue. Somebody claimed that water in a well near Yucaipa originated in the Sierra Nevada, coming down the Sierra Nevada fault system, and then coming down the San Andreas, and finally getting into a little branch fault and going over to the well in question. In short, they said that the water in the well originally came from the Sierra Nevada because they had earlier been enjoined from producing any further water from local sources. Benioff didn't believe that for a minute, nor did I. I got involved in the case, but did not enjoy that kind of activity.

Testifying as an expert witness is fascinating, but lawyers and scientists simply do not think the same way. Lawyers are certainly interested in "the truth," and the last thing they want you to do is not tell the truth. But they are not always interested in the whole truth. And college professors—particularly scientists—sometimes do not make very good expert witnesses in court cases. They want to ramble off and talk about the peripheral issues and about the pros and cons of different points of view. Another problem is that you lose control of your time because of court schedules. Particularly for someone whose primary responsibility

was teaching here at Caltech, I could not allow that to happen. After that one experience I decided I did not want to go further into forensic geology. So I avoided court cases, except when subpoenaed, as I was in a San Onofre case [see Chapter 7, Nuclear Concerns]. I did, however, get involved in controversies other than court cases. You might call them engineering cases; that is, they were good examples of significant engineering issues, usually not involving lawyers.

California Water Project

Allen: Hugo Benioff was chairman of the Consulting Board for Earthquake Analysis of the California Department of Water Resources, and I had gotten to know Benioff very well, partly because of my experience in helping him determine whether the Pacific Basin was rotating, which I have already described. Initially, the board was advising the department on the so-called Feather River Project that was then being planned and built as part of the California Water Project to bring water from northern to southern California. Subsequently, we helped them on all sorts of other water projects and on general issues of dam safety.

Hugo asked me if I would serve on the board, starting in 1963, shortly after it began. Other members of the board in 1963, besides Hugo Benioff (seismologist), were George Housner (structural engineer), Harry Seed (geotechnical engineer), Jim Sherard (dam engineer), and Nate Whitman (civil engineer). I think the board members considered some of the problems the water project faced to be more geological than they were prepared to handle, and that is why I was asked to come on the board. I was duly appointed to the board and am still on it to this day, some 38 years later. Hugo was chairman for a while, George Housner was chairman for a while, and I was chairman for almost ten years. I think that board has had a very constructive influence on the department.

Scott: What kind of help it has rendered?

Allen: The Consulting Board for Earthquake Analysis has been a very active board and, I think, very helpful in making sure that the state is up to par in terms of international practice. Indeed, the state of California has, over the years, led the way in many of those practices, such as in the regulation of dam safety with regard to earthquakes.

The routing of the State Water Project aqueduct was determined largely by the problem of fault crossings. They initially decided not to tunnel all the way from Bakersfield to Los Angeles. That might have been the cheapest thing to do, but since that would mean crossing the San Andreas fault at depth, they did not want to take that risk. So the routing was determined by the locations of crossings of the very active San Andreas and Garlock faults. They wanted the aqueduct to be near or at the surface where those crossings were made. They assumed, probably rightly, that either the Garlock fault or the San Andreas fault—the two major faults it crosses—will break during the life of the aqueduct, and they wanted to be in a position to make quick repairs. If it were deep underground, repair would be a much more difficult problem, particularly with major aftershocks going on for several years.

There was some precedent for doing this. The Metropolitan Water District of Southern California had also taken that approach earlier when it built the aqueduct from the Colorado River to southern California. One of the initial proposals had been to put it in a tunnel all the way. They decided not to do that for, I think, the same reason—they wanted to cross the San Andreas fault at the ground surface. One of their principal advisors on that had been Caltech's John Peter Buwalda, whom I mentioned before. A good deal of the Colorado River Aqueduct is located in tunnels. However, at the point where it crosses the San Andreas fault at Whitewater—the Banning branch of the fault—it is a covered canal at the ground surface. Whitewater is a few miles northwest of Palm Springs.

Still earlier, the Los Angeles Department of Water Resources had tunneled through the San Andreas fault at depth under Elizabeth Lake, west of Palmdale, when they brought Owens Valley water to Los Angeles. Thus far, they have not had the earthquake. But one of these days they will, and then it will be a real problem to repair the tunnel crossing at the point of a major fault offset, where it is several hundred feet underground.

In any event, the Consulting Board for Earthquake Analysis was a very stimulating group, as you can imagine, with members like Housner, Sherard, and Seed. Bruce Bolt came on later. The work of the board back in those earlier days was with the building of the California water system, whereas in recent years we have been called in much less often, mainly to advise on particular problems. This was the first time that a major engineering project had been built right next to a great fault and crossed the fault several times. A lot of pioneering thought went into this.

When they excavated for the embankment of Cedar Springs Dam, one of the California Aqueduct's major dams, they found that it would be sitting right on top of some significant faults that were obviously active because they displaced young stream gravels. Jim Sherard and I, in particular, became interested in this. The board recommended changing the dam's shape and lowering its height in response to the finding. Admittedly, of course, the dam is still built across the faults, but we think the amount of movement we might see would not be such as to cause dam failure.

Jim Sherard became quite interested in the problem of active faults in dam foundations —especially later, when he was consulting on dams all over the world. Stimulated by Sherard, Lloyd Cluff and I joined him in writing a paper on potentially active faults and dam foundations. I think that, to this day, there is a lot in the paper that could be of considerable interest to people building dams.[21]

Tarbela Dam, Pakistan

Allen: I have been involved in consulting on a variety of large dams and reservoirs in different parts of the world and will discuss a few examples here: Tarbela Dam in Pakistan, Aswan High Dam in Egypt, Itaipu Dam in Brazil-Paraguay, Auburn Dam in California, and the Three Gorges and Xiaolangdi Dams in China. I will also mention a number of other dams that help illustrate particular points I want to make.

21. Sherard, J.L, Cluff, L.S., and Allen, C.R., "Potentially Active Faults in Dam Foundations," *Geotechnique*. Vol. 24, p. 367-428, 1974.

I was involved in the Tarbela Dam in Pakistan for many years, starting in 1974, as a geological-seismological advisor. Tarbela Dam was and may still be the world's largest embankment dam. I became involved through an American engineering firm that was working on the design, because there was some suspicion of active faults directly beneath the dam. The designers wanted advice on whether the faults should be considered active, what kinds of earthquakes they might produce, and how often such earthquakes might happen.

Those are generally the questions on which I have given advice on many consulting jobs. Where are the faults that might affect the project, what kinds and what sizes of earthquakes might occur on these faults, and with what kinds of frequencies? The question of the exact nature of the ground shaking to be associated with the postulated earthquake is more of an engineering question—to be answered by geotechnical experts such as Harry Seed. I would tell them something like: "Consider a magnitude 7 earthquake 22 kilometers distant, of strike-slip type." From that, Harry Seed would go on to decide what the ground shaking would probably take place at the site itself. So the two fields are somewhat separate, although there is some overlapping. I would come in from the seismological end, and he and other geotechnical experts would come at it in the engineering sense.

In any event, Tarbela Dam turned out to be a fascinating situation, for a variety of reasons. As I say, active faults ran right underneath the structure, which had not been known when construction of the dam first got under way. In connection with drilling programs to understand the dam's foundation, a buried vertical escarpment was discovered that could only be explained by geologically recent faulting. On the other hand, the fault was not long enough to produce a truly great earthquake. Probably larger earthquakes could be produced by major thrust faults that underlie the whole region, and these were being considered anyway. One of my arguments was that even if an earthquake occurred on the newly discovered fault under the dam, it probably would not be as damaging as the regional earthquake for which the dam was already being designed. I have been back to Tarbela several times because the dam has come up for reevaluation. I have gotten to know some of the Pakistani geologists very well. It is a fascinating country and I have enjoyed working there.

Scott: In discussing Tarbela Dam and other foreign dams, say just a bit about the sources of information on which you made your judgments. Had pretty good geologic studies been done? Was there a useful literature? Did new studies have to be done in connection with the questions the consultants were trying to answer?

Allen: It was some of all of those. In every case, some geological work had already been done by local geologists, or by geologists hired by international firms involved in the dam design and construction. In many cases the geological work had been very well done, while in other cases it left much to be desired. In some cases new studies had to be done. We would ask that trenches be dug across a fault, or that further mapping be done, or aerial photographs be studied, and so forth. I should add that seismic hazard assessment is a very rapidly changing and a rapidly developing field, involv-

ing techniques almost unheard of a few years ago. Just because someone has been trained as a geologist, for example, doesn't mean that he or she is necessarily qualified to carry out the kinds of modern neotectonic studies that are often necessary nowadays.

As an advisor and consultant, however, for the most part you are not out there doing the field work yourself. Instead, you may recommend that a particular study be done. Sometimes the local work was done with amazing competency. Some of the Pakistani geologists did some very good work—much better than some of the work done by local geologists here in California. In China, very good work has been done in some cases, and in some cases dismal work. But I think that one reason consultants are brought in is to give differing and independent viewpoints on the nature of the evidence that is already available, and on the possible need for further backup. Still, it is hard to make generalizations on these responsibilities. In the case of faulting, very often I was using aerial photographs and doing some of the check-up work myself. But in all those cases, I think what I did was preceded and/or followed up by detailed work carried out by geologists and geophysicists hired by the international companies.

Aswan High Dam and Reservoir-Triggered Seismicity

Scott: Earlier you mentioned some of the other foreign dams you worked on.

Allen: Yes. A few years ago I became involved in a restudy of Aswan High Dam in Egypt. The restudy was being conducted by the geotechnical firm of Woodward-Clyde Consultants, with Harry Seed and Lloyd Cluff as the two principal leaders. At Aswan, we had a situation of suspected reservoir-triggered seismicity. This phenomenon had been recognized earlier at other major reservoirs, and I will speak more about this in connection with some other such structures.

Water had at that time never gone over the spillway at Aswan, since impoundment first started in 1964, but in the flood years of 1976-81 it reached significantly higher levels than had heretofore been attained, and earthquakes suddenly started to occur in 1981. Yet in the 4,000-year history of the Aswan area, there had never been any earthquakes of anywhere near the size of those that were starting to occur. This posed some questions. Were these earthquakes triggered by the presence of the reservoir? If so, what did that mean for the future of the dam? How well could it withstand the kinds of shaking that such earthquakes might produce?

It soon became clear that the earthquakes were indeed triggered by the reservoir. It is a little too complicated to go into here, but the final conclusion after two years of study by the consultants—during which I made several visits to Egypt—was that the maximum earthquake that could reasonably occur because of triggering would not cause major damage to the dam. I was not directly involved in studying the dam's stability—that is where Harry Seed and other consulting engineers came in—but I was involved in looking at the fault system where the earthquakes seemed to be occurring.

After that flurry of seismic activity, the water level went down again due to the Ethiopian drought, and when the water got low enough the earthquakes shut off at about the same water level where they had started. In 1997, the water

level reached that height again and has actually risen to spillway level at the dam. Although there was no reported immediate onset of earthquakes at the former critical level, it will be interesting to see if, with time and with the gradual readjustment of the underground hydrology, earthquakes do commence again.

Scott: You said the whole thing is complicated, but could you sketch the main outlines of your model in nontechnical terms? Why do you think the reservoir's presence triggers the quakes? Is it the weight of the water, or is there water seepage that maybe lubricates things down below, or what?

Allen: In most cases of reservoir-triggered seismicity, the activity starts almost immediately upon first impoundment of water. As the reservoir is filled, the earthquakes increase in magnitude, and in some cases the biggest earthquake occurs shortly after the water reaches spillway height. This has been true in a number of places such as Xinfengjiang Dam in China, and Koyna Dam in India. This pattern is pretty convincing. That is, in an area that has had no earthquake activity, the moment they start filling the reservoir, activity starts. As the reservoir gets fuller the activity increases until at the maximum water height you have the maximum earthquake. If the dam had been higher and the water able to go higher, they might have had still larger earthquakes.

We still call these "triggered" earthquakes, however, because so far as we can tell, the water does not *cause* the earthquakes, but rather it *triggers* the earthquakes. That is, the stresses are already there due to the mountain-building processes. But either water seeping down to depth or the weight of the water lowers the effective coefficient of friction and lets the stress cause the faulting on a preexisting fault. With larger reservoirs you have a greater weight of water, and probably greater seepage, and either one, or both in combination, may be able to trigger progressively larger earthquakes.

Scott: Somehow, the triggering mechanism worked in sort of a graduated fashion?

Allen: Yes, although the size of the earthquake also critically depends on the amount of stress that has been built up on the fault by long-term tectonic forces. Most large and deep reservoirs trigger no earthquakes at all, because there is evidently little tectonic strain present for them to "trigger."

Cases of delayed seismicity, like at Aswan, are much more difficult to evaluate than those where the triggered seismicity commences immediately upon the start of filling. Why did it wait until the water reached a certain height? The same was true of Oroville Dam here in California. Not until eight years after the dam was first filled did we have the Oroville earthquake—on a fault that goes right through the reservoir site. To this day we are not certain whether that earthquake was triggered by the reservoir, or would have happened anyway.

At Aswan High Dam, when the reservoir reached the high level I spoke of, for the first time it flooded a very wide area—a big embayment west of the main reservoir. Up until then, the embayment had been dry. When the water flooded the embayment, it got access to a very thick, porous sandstone bed that underlies much of western Egypt. Water essentially poured into this aquifer, completely changing

the hydrology and the earthquake potential. That was our hypothesis, based on the evidence. There was reason to say that at that particular time and water level, there was a major change in the earthquake-causation process.

Scott: Giving water access to the porous sandstone was part of the triggering mechanism?

Allen: Yes, it seems to make good sense. You will recall that Aswan High Dam was built by the Russians, and the chief Russian engineer was at the first meeting of our board. He was rather unhappy that anyone would question the dam's stability, and that was the last we saw of him. It is, in fact, a very conservatively built dam. Unfortunately, however, there were certain questions about what materials underlie certain parts of the dam, where we had to drill holes to make sample tests and draw the best conclusions we could. We concluded that the dam would be stable in the largest earthquake we could envisage occurring there. That is of course terribly important, and the Egyptian government was greatly concerned. Loss of Aswan High Dam would virtually mean the loss of Egypt.

Other Dams Where Triggering Has Been a Problem

Allen: I have been involved in a number of dams where triggered seismicity has been a problem. We still do not understand the phenomenon very well, and the whole problem is treated in greater detail in the recent book Bob Yeats, Kerry Sieh, and I wrote.[22] We would dearly love to drill a bunch of deep holes where a new dam is under construction, going down to the depth where earthquakes occur, and then measure the water-pore pressures there, but no one is willing to pay for that. So there are many fundamental aspects of the situation that we do not understand.

In particular, where dams are to be built and reservoirs impounded, we cannot confidently predict where triggered earthquakes will occur and where they won't. The great majority of large dams and reservoirs have not triggered earthquakes. Only a small number have done that. But we have not yet discovered how to say ahead of time what will happen. Thus, in the case of almost every deep reservoir, the dam has to be designed on the assumption that the reservoir can trigger a moderately large earthquake, even if the probability of that happening is maybe only 1 in 50, based on worldwide statistics of deep reservoirs.

In two cases, the reservoir impoundments triggered earthquakes of over magnitude 6 and centered right underneath the dams, and these almost brought the dams down. In Koyna, India, a large horizontal crack went right across the concrete dam, and but for the grace of God, the dam itself might have been lost. In Xinfengjiang Dam in China, another concrete dam, there was major cracking during a magnitude 6 earthquake. We now know that magnitude 6 earthquakes can cause very heavy local shaking. Fortunately, however, in neither case did they actually lose the dam, although there was significant loss of life in both instances that resulted from heavy shaking in nearby towns.

---

22. Yeats, R.S., Sieh, K., and Allen, C.R., *The Geology of Earthquakes.* Oxford University Press, New York. 568 pages, 1997. See particularly pages 466-471.

Scott: If those dams had been designed a little more conservatively, would the cracking probably have been avoided?

Allen: I am not an engineer, but my impression is that the answer is yes—it probably could have been avoided with more conservative engineering.

Scott: Have they been able to repair or retrofit those dams?

Allen: In the case of Xinfengjiang Dam, they started having earthquakes when impoundment first started. Fearing what might happen, the small earthquakes prompted them to redesign the dam and put some big buttresses on the downstream face. When the big one came, that measure probably saved the dam. I am not sure about Koyna, although the dam is apparently now back in service.

The first report of this triggering phenomenon anywhere in the world was at Lake Mead, in Nevada (Boulder/Hoover Dam). Back in the 1930s, a seismologist named Dean Carder suggested that earthquakes then occurring underneath Lake Mead were in fact triggered by the presence of the lake. The earthquakes were not very large—magnitude 5 or something like that—and did not cause any damage. But we did not have much of a seismographic record prior to the filling of the lake, so we are not really sure that the earthquakes were not happening quite independently of the dam and lake.

Itaipu Dam, Brazil-Paraguay

Allen: The Itaipu Dam on the Rio Paraná between Brazil and Paraguay is the biggest hydroelectric facility in the world and went into service in 1982. It was an interesting case because, although there was virtually no natural seismicity known in the area, several other smaller reservoirs in Brazil had produced minor triggered activity, even though no previous earthquakes had occurred in those areas either. The problem at Itaipu Dam was that it had to be filled very quickly, and sudden loading is what one worries about the most.

Scott: Why did it have to be filled quickly? Was it because there was such a volume of water flowing down the river?

Allen: It was an interesting situation. As I understand it, once the gates at the base of the dam were closed and filling commenced, they could not be reopened. There was then no way of releasing water from the reservoir until spillway level was reached. Meanwhile, the downstream channel would be left devoid of water except that coming in from downstream tributaries. The only way to guarantee sufficient downstream water in the main river was to carry out the operation during the flood season, when the downstream tributaries, such as the Iguaçú River below the famous falls, would deliver an adequate supply to the main channel.

Thus, they chose a flood period to fill one of the largest reservoirs in the world. The whole reservoir was filled in only nine days, and a lot of us had our fingers crossed. We had to tell them, "Yes, there is some probability that you might trigger seismic activity." I felt very relieved when that process was over, with no significant triggered event. Several people have demonstrated that periods of rapid filling or rapid draw-down are the most likely times to see triggered seismic activity. I helped set up the seismographic network at Itaipu, and so far

as I know, nothing of any concern has happened subsequent to the initial filling.

Auburn Dam, California

Allen: Auburn Dam was another interesting controversy in which I became involved, along with many other California earth scientists and engineers. I am sure you remember some of the hassle over it. I was on the consulting board appointed by the U.S. Bureau of Reclamation, which had become very alarmed when certain critics said that a dam of that particular proposed type—a thin-arch structure—should not be built in an area of potential earthquake activity. So the U.S. Bureau of Reclamation appointed the group on which I sat, and the state of California appointed another group independently.

The geology at the dam site was very complicated, but what turned out was that some of the faults in the region around the dam proved to be moderately active. The original assumption had been that there were no active faults anywhere near the dam. But later work, particularly by Woodward-Clyde Consultants, showed that there had been recent activity on many of the faults around the dam, some of them going almost through the dam's abutment.

Scott: As a member of the Seismic Safety Commission at the time, I was very much aware of that controversy, which was quite active around 1977 and 1978, not long after the Oroville earthquake. The commission got involved, at least to the extent of including the matter on the agendas of a number of its regular meetings. The Bureau of Reclamation staff would present the findings of their studies, particularly the work of Woodward-Clyde, and others would comment and raise questions.

Allen: Auburn was to be a doubly curved thin-arch dam, and would have been the world's longest structure of that type, had it been constructed. With that type of structure you did not want to have any fault displacement through the foundation. An embankment dam (of earth and rock) obviously can withstand some movement—maybe several feet—but only an inch or two of displacement might lead to great problems with a concrete thin-arch dam.

My recommendation was that they would have to assume that there could be a little displacement on a number of the faults that went beneath the dam, and I am still rather proud of my published analysis of the situation.[23] My conclusion was also echoed by a number of other people. The Bureau of Reclamation did not like that, because they had already invested half-a-billion dollars in the project. To change at that point to a completely different design that might better withstand fault displacement, such as an embankment dam, was effectively impractical for a variety of reasons. They were unhappy with most of their consultants' opinions, including mine, and may still be unhappy. It is not often that the consultants recommend something that goes so directly against what the contracting party wants to do, but that is, of course, exactly the reason for setting up a truly independent group of consultants.

The dam was not built, but it was a very interesting project that, I think, carried some les-

---

23. Allen, C.R., *Evaluation of the Seismic Hazard of the Auburn Dam Site, California.* Denver, U.S. Bureau of Reclamation, 1978.

sons. One lesson was, "If you are worried about seismic problems, you cannot confine yourself to mapping the geology of the dam site itself." The bureau had done a superb job of mapping the geology of the site itself, with detailed mapping of the exposed bedrock. But the worrisome clues came from looking at the surrounding regions within several miles of the site, where evidence was found of faults that had broken within the past 100,000 years.

Scott: At the time those studies were begun, my impression was that conventional geologic wisdom considered the Sierra foothill region pretty much seismically inactive. This changed after the 1975 Oroville earthquake, which was in the foothill region. The bureau's original geologic studies had not, however, looked beyond the Auburn dam site itself.

Allen: No, they had not looked beyond the site, although the later studies of Woodward-Clyde Consultants did look beyond. But the clear lesson was that you must do more than just look at the foundation itself. That is now becoming standard practice.

Scott: In other words, it is now well recognized that the geology of the surrounding region must also be considered?

Allen: Yes, it is now recognized that a broader approach is necessary to understand the overall seismic picture.

Xiaolangdi Dam, China

Allen: Two very large dams are under construction in China, the Xiaolangdi Dam on the Yellow River, and the Three Gorges Dam on the Yangtze River. Both are big rivers, and floods have occurred throughout China's history, particularly on the Yellow River, causing tremendous tragedies on the plains of east China.

Because the Yellow River dam is a World Bank project, the Chinese had to set up an international consulting board. The World Bank selected Ed Idriss, of the University of California at Davis, and me to be the two Americans on the board the Chinese set up in 1990. At the first two meetings of the board in China, however, it turned out that the level of earthquake shaking that we, Ed Idriss and I, recommended was a little higher than the local Chinese groups had recommended for the Xiaolangdi Dam.

Ed was not satisfied that the design was adequate to withstand the earthquake ground motions, based on the evidence we had at that time. So we requested further investigations and a demonstration that the dam's design was adequate. This was in about 1991, and neither of us has been back since. The dam site is the last place downriver where it would be possible to construct a dam, and if it should fail, perhaps 100 million lives are at stake in the entire flood plain. Insofar as I am aware, the dam is still under construction, although perhaps with a modified board of consultants.

Scott: Is the dam's main purpose flood control? What about water storage for irrigation, or power?

Allen: It would provide power, but that was not the only purpose. The big problem is that the Yellow River brings down so much sediment that they have had to build dikes out across the plains of China to contain the river. So the river now flows at a higher level than the plains around it. As more and more sediments are deposited, the dikes have had to be built

higher and higher. One purpose of the dam was to catch some of the sediment, so they would not have to keep raising the dikes. Everyone understood that this dam was not a permanent solution, but I believe they considered it cheaper to build the dam than to have to keep raising the dikes for the next 40 years.

Scott: I believe the name of the Yellow River comes from the prevailing color of the water, due to the heavy sediment load picked up when it traverses regions of highly erodible loess deposits.

Allen: Yes, it is probably the most silt-laden large river in the world. At least one large dam farther upstream has had to be virtually abandoned because of filling of the reservoir by sediments.

Three Gorges Dam, China

Allen: The Yangtze River, on which the Three Gorges Dam is being built, is a bigger river than the Yellow, but does not have as concentrated a sediment load. The purpose of the project is primarily for power generation. It started out as a World Bank project, but I believe the World Bank was unhappy with some of the environmental aspects of the reservoir, particularly in the upstream area that would be affected by the stored water. When the World Bank pulled out, the Chinese went ahead on their own, and I believe the dam is now being built entirely with Chinese financing.

I was involved only because of an argument between some of the parties there about one of the faults near the dam. I was asked to come over, sort of as a visitor but with my way paid, to help resolve the dispute, or at least to give my opinion on the degree of activity of this particular fault. I am not a formal consultant on the dam, and there may not be any foreign consultants on it at all. The Chinese have lots of expertise in building dams—they have built big dams all over China. It is not a Third World country when it comes to those skills.

Scott: Say a little more about the earthquake fault in question, and the outcome.

Allen: The questions were: Was the suspected fault active, and should the dam be designed on the assumption that the fault could produce a significant earthquake? On the basis of my very brief visit, I did not consider the fault to be active, and some of the claims of instrumentally measured slow movements on the fault were not credible to me. Furthermore, the suspect fault was located some distance away from the dam site—about ten kilometers, as I recall—and it was not a long or tectonically important structure. So, even if there were to be an earthquake on the fault, it would probably not produce shaking at the dam of sufficient intensity to consider in the design. Basically, the Three Gorges site is in a geologically very stable area, which cannot be said of the Xiaolangdi site on the Yellow River.

Scott: So you sided with one group in the controversy over the fault's activity. What happened then?

Allen: I haven't followed the situation in detail, but insofar as I know, the fault is no longer a significant issue.

Eastside Reservoir Project, California

Allen: Finally, let me mention my recent activities—primarily since becoming an emeritus professor in 1990—as a member of the Board of Consultants for the Eastside Reservoir Project of the Metropolitan Water District of Southern California. [The completed reservoir is now known as Diamond Valley Reservoir.] Located near Hemet, roughly 75 miles southeast of Los Angeles, this is the largest dam construction project underway in the United States, with contracts totaling more than a billion dollars. Serving on the board with me are Ed Idriss, Rich Kramer, Tom Leps, Al O'Neill, and Bill Wallace, representing expertise in geotechnical engineering, dam design, engineering geology, hydraulic structures, and electrical power engineering.

The project is a complex one that involves two large dams, one at each end of a formerly dry valley. Also involved are a moderately large saddle dam on the rim of the valley, as well as a major outlet structure, pumping plant, and several adits and tunnels. As I understand it, the purpose of the reservoir is to add to the storage of water in southern California in order to balance supplies during wet and dry years. No "new" water is involved, only better use of water now being delivered from northern California and the Colorado River.

Another important consideration is that it will provide further water storage south of the main San Andreas fault system, in case a major earthquake cuts off imported water supplies to southern California for a period of perhaps a year or more.

My presence on the board is probably due to concerns by the district, as well as by the public, that the project is located squarely within the plexus of faults lacing through southern California. There were two principal seismic hazard concerns: Were there any faults actually within the reservoir or under the proposed dams themselves, and, even if not, what kinds of maximum earthquakes should be considered on the nearby San Andreas fault, as well as its major branches even closer to the site, the San Jacinto and Elsinore faults?

The board carefully followed work by geotechnical consultants investigating suspected active faults near and through the reservoir, but there was convincing evidence that none of these local faults had moved during the past few tens of thousands of years, based on analyses of soils exposed in trenches excavated across the suspect features. But then, somewhat of a surprise occurred during excavation of the foundation for the West Dam—the larger of the two major structures—when one fault was found breaking the stream-channel gravels directly under the centerline of the projected dam. Intensive study of this fault finally showed that it indeed displaced the older, deeper gravels, but that the breaks were truncated by unbroken younger gravels that themselves had an age of probably several hundred thousand years. Thus, the fault had not broken within the past several hundred thousand years, clearly taking it out of the "active" category.

Considerable field effort was carried out by a number of district geologists and consultants to document these relationships, and many trenches were excavated and samples taken. This effort demonstrates the need for state-of-the-art studies that are now often necessary to satisfy owners and regulators—not to speak of the general public, which in this day and age is inevitably kept aware of ongoing studies and controversies by the news media. All in all, the Metropolitan Water District handled this rather delicate situation very well, and I hope that my presence on the consulting board helped in guiding the field studies and in giving credibility to the district's conclusions.

Matahina Dam, New Zealand

Allen: A project that started only a few years ago and was recently completed is the strengthening of Matahina Dam in New Zealand. I served on a Board of Review, together with U.S. engineers Skip Hendron and Eric Kollgaard, to advise the Electricity Corporation of New Zealand (ECNZ) on the remediation project. The dam, whose purpose is solely for electric power production, lies on the Rangitaiki River near the north coast of New Zealand's North Island. Although the dam was built only in the 1950s, the impervious core of the embankment structure has suffered minor damage twice, once in connection with settling shortly after the dam was built, and then because of shaking by a fairly major nearby earthquake in 1987. During the initial construction, when the foundation was excavated down to bedrock, it was observed that several faults parallel to the river valley underlay the dam, although nothing was known about their degree of activity.

Now we realize that these faults represent the northern, fraying-out end of the Alpine fault system, which has generated major historic earthquakes in central New Zealand, several hundred miles to the south. Particularly with modern techniques now available to study the degree of activity of faults, ECNZ felt it prudent to reevaluate the safety of the dam, particularly with respect to the faults underlying the structure. The principal questions were: Were the faults underlying the dam active? What were the maximum earthquakes that might reasonably be expected to occur on them? What kinds of fault displacements might be expected to be associated with the maximum earthquakes? How often? And then, if there was cause for concern, what type of engineering remediation might be appropriate?

A joint American-New Zealand geologic team excavated numerous trenches across various branches of the fault at distances up to 40 km from the dam, and many coreholes were drilled and geologic mapping was carried out in the attempt to understand the detailed fault configuration at and near the site. Unfortunately, of course, many critical exposures lay buried beneath the reservoir and the dam itself. A unique advantage here, however, as compared to many similar projects, was that the local volcanic ash stratigraphy was well known from earlier academic studies, so that fault offsets in trench walls could be well dated. To make a long story short, it was concluded by the team—and the Board of Review agreed—that the fault was sufficiently active so that future large earthquakes on it could not be ruled out, and that such events could pose a significant hazard to the dam because of possible fault offsets through its core.

But rehabilitating or strengthening a dam is not a simple matter, particularly when faced with possible fault offsets, and ECNZ and the board

looked at many alternatives. One option was simply to get rid of the dam and reservoir altogether, but this was not considered viable in view of the cost and effort of environmental restoration. The option finally chosen was to place a major rock buttress on the downstream flank of the dam, together with other additions and modifications, with the objective of avoiding catastrophic downstream flooding if there was significant fault offset through the structure. In other words, after the maximum earthquake, the dam might not still be completely functional, but there would have been no significant danger to downstream residents or property. I emphasize that fault offset through the dam was judged to be very unlikely during its service life, but still sufficiently credible to warrant protection for the potentially affected public.

I mention this project because similar issues will undoubtedly be arising worldwide as we learn more about earthquakes and their effects, as well as about the earthquake resistance of various types of existing structures. In the 1994 Northridge earthquake, for example, we saw that the intensity of ground shaking exceeded that which many people had expected, and, at the same time, the behavior of one class of steel buildings was not up to what had been expected. Strengthening or rehabilitation of existing structures is a major engineering challenge, with both economic and political ramifications. And the old question of how safe is "safe enough" harks back to the geologist's and seismologist's ability to quantify what the hazard really is.

Chapter 7

Nuclear Concerns: Power Plants and Waste Disposal

*It has been very interesting because
it involved quite a bit of politics as
well as science.*

Nuclear Power Plants: San Onofre and Diablo Canyon

Allen: Although I have indicated a general reluctance to get
embroiled in nuclear power plant issues, I did get involved in
two nuclear projects in California. One involvement, with San
Onofre, was only minor. I had purposely stayed largely out of
that because of the reservations I mentioned earlier. But then I
was subpoenaed by the Friends of the Earth to come down to a
Nuclear Regulatory Commission (NRC) hearing at San Clem-
ente and testify. I went as a somewhat unwilling witness. I was
not an "unfriendly" witness, but I would not have gone except
for the subpoena.

There was a great debate on the seismic hazard at San Onofre.
It was interesting to discover that the lawyers for the Friends of
the Earth were much less effective than the lawyers for the
Southern California-Edison Company, which was the applicant.

Although it was not the Friends' lawyers intent when they had me subpoenaed, and it was not my purpose in going down there, I think my testimony ended up helping Southern California Edison more than the Friends of the Earth.

Scott: Was that largely due to more astute questioning by the Southern California Edison lawyers?

Allen: Yes. I had not gone down there with the idea of either criticizing or defending the proposed plant. The Friends of the Earth had obviously hoped I would say something that would help them. And if they had asked the right questions, I perhaps could have helped them. But the Edison lawyers were just a lot sharper. Anyway, that was a one-day venture for me on that nuclear plant.

I did, however, get very deeply involved in the reevaluation of the Diablo Canyon nuclear plant operated by the Pacific Gas & Electric Company near San Luis Obispo, California. When it was built, there was a lot of controversy about the seismic hazard, but I was not involved and, again, had purposely stayed out. One of the conditions of the license granted by the Nuclear Regulatory Commission, however, was that at a later date PG&E carry out an extensive seismic study over a period of some five years, to see if anything had changed in our understanding of the seismic hazard. What had we learned in the interim?

I was involved in this second go-round as a member of a PG&E board, which included many of the same people I have already talked about—Harry Seed, Bruce Bolt, and others. That was a very interesting experience because we had the opportunity to recommend spend-

ing lots of money on some important studies. These studies had a strong emphasis on seismological research, as well as on the safety of the specific site. For example, PG&E put out a dense seismographic network. PG&E also did a lot of geomorphic studies—studies of the local physiography—because the reactor site is on a marine terrace that has been uplifted by tectonic activity. One of the questions was: When did that uplift take place?

There was another even more important question: Was that marine terrace deformed in a way that suggests the presence of underlying blind thrust faults? One of the clues to a blind thrust deep in the earth is that it tends to deform the surface by folding. That is true at places like Whittier Narrows or Northridge, where we have had blind-thrust earthquakes. The team was able to demonstrate that the terrace at Diablo Canyon—which extends for many miles in almost a U-shape around the plant—is completely undeformed. That gave us confidence that active blind thrusting was not a problem underneath the plant.

On the other hand, the Hosgri fault, three or four kilometers from the shoreline and the reactor, had long been recognized as a problem, having been discovered when they were part way through the initial construction. We did a lot of work to try to understand that fault's degree of activity, what the sense of motion might be, what the likelihood of an earthquake was, and those types of things. It was a very interesting and thorough study. No one denies the fault being capable of generating a large earthquake. But as a result of our work, the NRC accepted the recommendation that the plant continue to operate, PG&E having demonstrated that the plant would be safe, even during a very large earthquake on the Hosgri fault. As I recall, the Hosgri fault was considered capable of generating about a magnitude 7 earthquake.

Scott: So, the nuclear facility had been designed for that much shaking?

Allen: I believe it was upgraded after the Hosgri fault was first discovered. At that time, there may have been some modification of the plant. I am not an expert on that. But I do not think they had to do any further upgrading as a result of our later studies.

Fortunately, by the time I was involved, the issue was not nearly as emotional as it had been earlier. There were still intervenors—people who were opposed to the plant—and scientists who disagreed with members of the PG&E team. But for the most part, these discussions were carried on in a civil and constructive way. At the end of the PG&E study, the NRC approved continued operation of the plant. To this day there are still differences of opinion on the issue, but they are not nearly as emotional as were some of the earlier fights.

Radioactive Waste Disposal

Allen: I have become involved in a number of projects of the National Academy of Sciences, and can talk more about some of them later. The one I want to mention now is the Board on Radioactive Waste Management, on which I began serving in 1985. I think I was asked to serve because in many people's minds earthquakes and volcanoes represent a major problem in any potential nuclear waste repository,

particularly in the western U.S. And indeed, they are hazards that have to be considered.

Probably the most significant work of that group during my tenure on it was publication of a report calling for more flexibility both in thinking about high-level radioactive waste disposal, and in the bureaucracy of the investigative and licensing process. Over the years, I think that brief report has had more impact on a variety of agencies and groups than that of any other committee of the National Academy of Sciences on which I have served. I was on that board for several years, until 1991.[24]

Nuclear Waste Technical Review Board

Allen: In the late 1980s, Congress passed legislation setting up the Nuclear Waste Technical Review Board, an independent government agency to advise the secretary of energy and the Congress on the technical aspects of the proposed repository site at Yucca Mountain, about 100 miles north of Las Vegas, Nevada. The members were nominated by the National Academy of Sciences, and appointed by the President. In 1989, I was appointed by President Reagan as one of the eleven members of the board, and served until I completed my second 4-year term in 1997.

I found the work very interesting, because the technical problems of disposing of nuclear wastes are indeed very challenging. And, particularly at Yucca Mountain, you have to be con-

24. Parker, F.L., Allen, C.R., and 16 others, *Rethinking High-Level Radioactive Waste Disposal.* National Academy Press, Washington D.C. 38 p., 1990.

cerned with earthquakes and volcanoes. Many people do not realize that a small volcanic cone, less than 100,000 years old, is only about six miles from the proposed repository site.

It has been very interesting because it involved quite a bit of politics as well as science. The site has been vehemently opposed by the state of Nevada, as well as by many citizens of the Las Vegas region, and the politics have gotten pretty hot and heavy at times. The acceptance or rejection of the Yucca Mountain site may eventually be decided, not primarily by technical issues, but instead by congressional mandate. The interaction between science and politics has been intriguing to me, but it's obviously frustrating to the scientists who have devoted large parts of their careers to scientific investigations of the site, where a lot of excellent work has been done. There have also been some interesting scientific surprises, particularly in the way in which water apparently flows through the mountain.

Scott: You mentioned that the Nuclear Waste Technical Review Board is an independent government agency. Would you describe it?

Allen: It's an independent agency with a total membership of about 22 people, including support staff. We report to the Secretary of Energy and to the Congress, but we are completely independent and are not at all an adjunct of the Department of Energy. We had to set up our own bookkeeping and logistical support. The board meets four times a year, but subcommittees meet much more often than that. I think our Technical Review Board has been very constructive. We have been quite critical of the DOE at times and very complimentary at other

times, but I think it is a much better program because of our actions on it. Membership on the board was a very interesting experience for me.

In my opinion, nuclear waste disposal is a terribly important national and international problem, and we simply have to face up to it. Most members of the public certainly do not want a repository to be located near them—the NIMBY (Not In My Back Yard) syndrome. Although this attitude is understandable, many people would apparently just as soon leave this very dangerous high-level waste where it is now—stored at more than 100 nuclear power plants and defense installations around the country. But this is not a viable long-term solution, for a variety of reasons, and we simply must face up to a permanent answer in the not-too-distant future.

Many plants are running out of storage space, and maintaining security at decommissioned plants is a serious problem that will only get worse with time. Also, there is the ethical argument: Our generation caused the problem, and we should do something about it—not leave it for future generations. We must recognize, at the same time, that many anti-nuclear activists are working against *any* solution of the waste disposal problem, in the hope that this stalemate will prevent construction of any more nuclear power plants in the future and perhaps lead to early shutdowns of currently operating plants.

Scott: I take it you think the problem could be solved if we could deal with the political issues?

Allen: Yes. While it is a very difficult problem *technically*, I think it is solvable, in terms of finding a place that is adequately safe. Some concerns have been raised recently about criticality and so forth, but I am convinced that there is a technical solution. I am optimistic, although certainly not assured, that the Yucca Mountain site will eventually be found technically suitable. But I don't know whether we will be able to resolve the political aspect of the problem.[25]

Scott: Say a little more about your optimism that the problem is technically solvable. Are studies underway [at time of interview in 1996] that you think ought to provide reasonable technical assurance regarding the Yucca Mountain site?

Allen: The Department of Energy has recently completed a tunnel into the area of the proposed site, so we can actually get down there more than a thousand feet and see what those rocks look like at the proposed repository level. While we have already drilled a lot of holes, there are certain things we do not know. There are a lot of faults there, and we do not now know to what extent some of these faults are open and could possibly carry water. To my mind, water drainage through the system is the most serious problem.

Scott: The main concern is that the waste could escape its containers and the drainage might take it out of the repository and into the groundwater?

Allen: Right. You have to assume that over thousands of years the canisters enclosing the radioactive spent fuel will lose much of their

---

25. In July 2002, Congress and the President approved the Yucca Mountain site over the veto of the state of Nevada. As of fall 2002, the repository has yet to obtain a license from the Nuclear Regulatory Commission, which will involve several more years of intensive investigation.

integrity. And much to many people's surprise, it turns out that the faults on both sides of the Yucca Mountain site—which is a fault block—have had displacements within the past 10,000 years. In other words, by many people's definition they are active.

Clearly the movements must have been related to earthquakes. Some opponents and members of the public think that this automatically disqualifies the site, but I cannot agree. We can design the facility for any kind of shaking we want to impose on it. We are not talking about a nuclear power plant with all its complications. Instead, there will simply be a bunch of buried stainless steel canisters.

I am not nearly as concerned about the earthquake problem as I am with the hydrology: the water flow through the site and how the water flow might be affected by faults going through the rocks. For that we need to know what the faults look like at depth, and what the water transmissibility really is. The current big effort is on that issue. [Since the time of this interview in 1996, considerable further progress has been made.]

Let me end with an observation or two that might add a little human interest and humor, and which are also relevant to the frustrations of serving on governmental committees. I mentioned earlier that I had originally been appointed to the Nuclear Waste Technical Review Board by President Reagan, but I was reappointed to a second 4-year term by President George Bush.

In connection with my reappointment to the board by the Bush White House in 1992, three amusing incidents are perhaps indicative of the growing bureaucracy in government advisory bodies—even those of a completely nonpolitical nature. Although earlier in my career I had been through several military security screenings and Q-clearance procedures, nothing approached the scrutiny I was subjected to in connection with this reappointment. As usual, my neighbors were interviewed, and an FBI agent asked the woman across the hall in my condominium—not unexpectedly—whether she was aware of any substance abuse to which I was prone. She apparently responded, "Oh yes, I know that Dr. Allen is addicted to artichokes," whereupon he took on a dire and menacing look and said, "Lady, this is not funny!"

Later, near the end of the clearance procedure, I was called by probably the same FBI agent and asked—still one more time—the typical list of questions about foreign associates, personal matters, and organizational affiliations. Finally, he said in a completely deadpan tone-of-voice, "I have just one further question. Dr. Allen, when is the Big One coming?"

And then, after apparent FBI approval, I was called by a woman in the White House Personnel Office and asked what my political party affiliation was. I rather resented the question, not only because I thought it was irrelevant, but because it was already a matter of written record on forms I had filled out, as well as being in the public record. But I respectfully reported that I was a registered Democrat. She paused at length, and then finally replied, "Well, maybe we can get you reappointed anyway!" I was, in fact, reappointed by President Bush.

Chapter 8

Significant Scientific Papers

. . . most scientists would like to think that they leave their mark on the world primarily through their publications, although the inspiration of students also ranks very highly.

Scott: I hope you will review a selection of your articles and publications which—in your own opinion—have been the most significant. The oral history of a scientist like you would be incomplete without some attention given to writings and contributions to the literature.

Allen: You're right, and most scientists would like to think that they leave their mark on the world primarily through their publications, although the inspiration of students also ranks very highly. And I don't mean to downplay contributions to public policy. From some 150 scientific papers that I have published, let me pick out for special discussion about ten, some of which I have mentioned briefly earlier in these interviews.

Scott: In the process, you can explain their significance in terms that nontechnical readers and people in other disciplines can understand.

Glaciological Work

Allen: Although I was a structural geologist, after I got my Ph.D. I spent quite a bit of time doing glaciological work, particularly because of the influence of Bob Sharp, whom I mentioned earlier. We worked in Alaska and Canada, and on Mt. Olympus in the state of Washington. One resulting paper, on the Blue Glacier in Washington, was published in 1960.[26]

What I did was study ice as a kind of deformed rock. After all, ice is by definition a rock, but it deforms relatively rapidly, the way rocks do over very great time periods. Some very interesting structures develop in a glacier that give you clues as to what has gone on. As you look at the lower end of a glacier, you see clues as to what kinds of mechanical processes have taken place between what you see down there and what originally started as snow way up in the ice field. I tried to map the glacier ice as I would map a metamorphic rock—and it was the first time, or one of the first times, this had been done. A metamorphic rock has been through change—it usually has foliation (lamination) and planes of weakness. Similarly, the ice in a glacier is not like the block of ice that we used to see the iceman deliver, but it also has foliation, bubbles, and features that represent the deformational history. I made hundreds of observations on the surface of the Blue Glacier, noting the foliation, where the shear zones were, the orientations of crevasses, and

so forth. I ended up with a map that looked like a very detailed geologic map of rock terrain.

Scott: You mentioned foliation. What is that?

Allen: Foliation (lamination) results when ice is sheared. When ice is going downhill very rapidly it tends to shear because some parts of the ice stream are moving more rapidly than others. For example the Blue Glacier, on which I was working, was fed by two main ice streams, which came over two separate icefalls and then coalesced into a single glacier about halfway down the mountain. Each of these icefalls gave its own characteristic patterns to the ice, with a zone in between where there was exceptionally intense shearing.

Many people have referred to our paper on that work as the first attempt to use rigorous geologic mapping to understand the mechanics of how the ice changes in coming from the ice field to the toe of a glacier. I did that together with others, of course, but I was the lead author and am rather proud of the paper. When your name is Allen, it often appears first in a list of multiple authors. Sometimes this is for alphabetical reasons, and at other times I really was the lead investigator.

Scott: How did you map the glacier, and what did you learn?

Allen: I used field geologic techniques—when I went out on the glacier, for example, I had a typical compass and inclinometer. One of the problems was locating my position on the glacier. Fortunately, we had surveyed-in an array of stakes while watching how the glacier moved from year to year. We knew where the stakes were, so I could always refer myself to the stakes, and I also used aerial photographs.

26. Allen, C.R., Kamb, W.B., Meier, M.F., Sharp, R.P., "Structure of the Lower Blue Glacier, Washington," *Journal of Geology*. Vol. 68, p. 601-625, 1960.

Unfortunately, for that purpose of course, the glacier changes with time.

The principal thing we discovered was that, although the glacier in its lower reaches was one tongue of ice, it consisted of two completely different structures, each representing one of the two original ice fields and the individual icefalls over which those two streams had come. They then joined in a very complicated septum we somewhat jokingly called the "Gesundheitstrasse"—*not* a good German word, but reflecting to some degree the very great complications of this zone.

What were the significant impacts of what we learned? I think we developed a better feel for the way in which ice flows. In addition, we were drilling holes to the bottom of the glacier to measure how the surface moved relative to the base, and what velocity gradient it had. Others of our research group—Bob Sharp in particular—were leading in those studies, although I was helping on that project too. Barclay Kamb was using an ingenious optical device to study the nature and deformation of ice crystals at various depths in the glacier, from cores recovered from the drill holes.

Some people asked why it was important to know how ice flows, but we found that among the people who were most interested were the metallurgists. In metallurgy, one has the problem of how metals change with temperature, yielding, annealing, and so forth. But metal is not transparent, whereas ice is. Ice also has the advantage of being monomineralic—composed of just one mineral. So, strangely enough, many of the early studies of the deformation of ice had been done by metallurgists trying to get a better idea of how one crystal grows at the

expense of another. How does flowage actually take place? Do some crystals get smaller as others get larger? These were the kinds of questions we were trying to deal with. I was among the coauthors of a more general summary paper published several years later, after a number of further field seasons on the Blue Glacier.[27]

Study of Faulting in Philippines-Taiwan Region

Allen: In 1962, I published a paper on circum-Pacific faulting in the Philippines-Taiwan region. I referred to this earlier when talking about working with Hugo Benioff when he was hoping to find, but did not find, strike-slip faults that were right-lateral in displacement and which would support his idea of a rotating Pacific Basin.[28]

This was one of the first times I went off into the boondocks to do field geology, doing it with the help of local geologists, of course. Particularly in foreign countries, one has to get the cooperation and help of local geologists, and not incur their ire at some foreign geologists coming in and wanting to steal all of their best data. The work in the Philippines was very interesting because much of it was in areas that were rather remote. We did a lot of walking, hiking, jeep driving, airplane flying, and so forth, much of it in areas then controlled—at

---

27. Meier, M.F., Kamb, W.B., Allen, C.R., and Sharp, R.P., "Flow of Blue Glacier, Olympic Mountains, Washington," *Journal of Glaciology*. Vol. 68, p. 187-212, 1974.

28. Allen, C.R., "Circum-Pacific Faulting in the Philippines-Taiwan Region," *Journal of Geophysical Research*. Vol. 67, p. 4795-4812, 1962.

least at night—by the Huks, which you may remember as a post-war guerilla group.

In contrast to most of my other foreign studies, the resulting paper has no local coauthors because I worked with such a great number and variety of local people in both the Philippines and Taiwan. That paper has stood the test of time. I mentioned earlier that other geologists have subsequently claimed that the sense of displacement on the Philippine fault was different from what I had claimed, and it turned out I was right.

Scott: Was your main intent to determine the direction of movement on the faults?

Allen: Of course, the principal stimulus was to determine the relative motion, if any, between the Pacific Ocean and the western Pacific rim. There was, first of all, a basic question as to whether or not there was actually such a fault in the Philippines. At the time, there was just sort of a hint in the literature that there might be. I was hoping there would be something similar to the San Andreas. Indeed, before I went there I looked at a lot of maps and aerial photographs and concluded that there probably was a continuous feature. It turned out that the Philippine fault is a major strike-slip fault, very comparable to the San Andreas, but not quite as long.

Scott: I presume vegetation is one reason why it is not as obvious or easy to find as the San Andreas fault, which goes through semi-arid territory for much of its length?

Allen: Vegetation certainly makes a difference. Also, in the Philippines, it was complicated by volcanism and some other factors, such as the fact that many segments of the fault

are buried beneath the oceanic waters separating the various Philippine islands. In any event, the initial effort was just to determine whether there was a fault there or not, which was a matter of some debate. Second, I wanted to determine the sense of displacement. Third, I wanted to determine its degree of activity. That would fit into the overall seismic hazard analysis of the Philippines. The fault turned out to be reasonably active. In fact, the 1990 earthquake on the fault in central Luzon, which I mentioned earlier, led to the deaths of almost 2,000 people.

Today, of course, we have newer techniques to study and get quantitative data on the degree of a fault's activity. But then we relied on such clues as the fact that stream channels crossing the fault were offset horizontally. Moreover, they were consistently offset in one direction, indicating left-lateral movement. In geologic terms, stream channels are very ephemeral features of the earth's surface. Unless the fault has a reasonably high degree of activity, features such as stream offsets will not be preserved—streams will simply erode through the barrier caused by the horizontal displacement on the fault, and they will then continue downhill in a relatively straight line instead of being offset at the fault.

So, the consistent offsets along the Philippine fault were evidence of a relatively high degree of activity in very recent geologic time. I found similar offset stream channels—again left-handed—along a major fault extending some 100 miles parallel to Taiwan's eastern coast. There, however, a major earthquake on this fault in 1951 had produced well-documented left-handed displacements, particularly through a school building in Yuli, so there was not the excitement of discovery and exploration that accompanied the study of the Philippine fault to the south.

1965 Paper on Seismicity and Geologic Structure

Allen: Another important contribution, in my opinion, was the 1965 paper by myself, Pierre St. Amand, Charles Richter, and John Nordquist on the relationship between seismicity and geologic structure in southern California. St. Amand had been a fellow graduate student with me here at Caltech, and I had worked with him in Chile. Richter is well-known, and Nordquist was a senior technician at the Seismological Laboratory here.[29]

For what I believe was the first time, this paper pulled together evidence on the nature of the geologic structure where earthquakes occurred. That is, we looked at the faults, tried to get some idea of their degree of activity, and compared that with the seismological data on where earthquakes were now occurring. We did a lot of computer work. Back at the time, we were using IBM cards, trying to sum the amount of energy or strain release in various parts of southern California. We made maps showing where energy had been primarily released during earthquakes and compared that with the geologic structures as we knew them from geologic mapping.

29. Allen, C.R., St. Amand, P., Richter, C.F., and Nordquist, J.M., "Relationship between Seismicity and Geologic Structure in the Southern California Region," *Seismological Society of America Bulletin*. Vol. 55, p. 753-797, 1965.

I believe some of our conclusions were very important. One conclusion was that almost all the big earthquakes in southern California were related to faults that could be seen on the ground's surface. That seems fairly obvious today, although we have the added complication of now knowing that there are some blind faults that do not reach the surface, but yet can produce earthquakes such as the 1994 Northridge, California earthquake. Nevertheless, the great bulk of earthquakes have been associated with faults that are visible at the surface.

It also turns out that small earthquakes do not necessarily occur where big ones do. Our feeling was that if we simply got better seismographs, we would find that all the earthquakes would end up being located on major faults. But, in fact, we found that the occurrence of small earthquakes is very widespread in southern California, and their distribution is not necessarily indicative of where large earthquakes occur. Small earthquakes occur on faults, almost by definition, but in many cases these may just be minor cracks. Of course in some places, as along the San Jacinto fault, there is a great cloud of small earthquake activity. But there are also small earthquakes in other parts of southern California in locations that have not had a large earthquake in historic times and may never experience such an event.

This was the kind of information we were trying to pull together. It was sort of the culmination of my desire to try to bring the different approaches together, which had not been done previously. We did this at the Seismological Laboratory, which traditionally had been solely a seismological organization. A lot of it had to do with geology, not seismology, and Richter was very supportive of the effort to blend the two.

Scott: So you considered the seismological data as well as the geology of the regions where earthquakes were occurring?

Allen: Yes. Not only the geology that we had mapped, but also geology as reported by other people and as turned up by literature searches. Also, for the first time, we went back and tried to catalog in a systematic way California earthquakes whose locations had been documented by our seismographic system here, which started back about 1927. We gathered all this information together, and computerized it to see what areas had been more active than others, whether there had been changes, and so forth. That 1965 paper is still being referred to in the literature.

1967 Paper on Tectonic Environments

Allen: In 1967, I wrote a paper on seismic environments along the San Andreas fault system, which I prepared for a conference on earthquakes and structure in California held at Stanford. It was not published in a major journal, but in a Stanford University publication series that is almost in the "gray" literature, a term we use to refer to publications, often miscellaneous reports and conference proceedings that, although printed, are not easy to come by in many libraries.[30] The paper was not a partic-

---

30.   Allen, C.R., "The Tectonic Environments of Seismically Active and Inactive Areas Along the San Andreas Fault System," *Stanford University Publications in the Geological Sciences*. Vol. 11, p. 70-82, 1967.

ularly long piece, but in it I had an idea that sort of caught on, so the paper has been quoted widely for that one idea.

Sometime earlier we had discovered fault creep in California, places where the San Andreas fault was moving gradually with time, rather than abruptly during big earthquakes. Karl Steinbrugge first discovered this near Hollister, where it caused some consternation in the insurance industry as to whether or not it was "earthquake-related." We knew that creep was limited to some areas of the fault. Certain parts of the San Andreas fault are locked, and have been for at least a hundred years, judging from undeformed old fences of known age that cross the fault in many places. Other parts of the fault are moving gradually. The question is why? What is different? One of the arguments was that the parts that were creeping were either doing so because this was premonitory to a great earthquake on that part of the fault, or maybe it represented some sort of creep that followed the last great prehistoric earthquake on that part of the fault.

Some people claimed, and perhaps some still do, that the creeping segments are temporal. That is, creeping represents one phase in the life of the fault, and is taking place either prior to or following a great earthquake, or perhaps both. There is good reason to suspect that, because in laboratory work when testing the failure of materials, very often there is a gradual slip, sort of a premonitory slip, just before a sudden failure. It starts out slowly, and then, bang, there is complete failure.

I observed that the part of the San Andreas fault that was creeping was the segment where the so-called Franciscan rock was found on one side of the fault. The Franciscan rock sequence in California is a very important sequence. It was laid down many millions of years ago and includes many volcanic components. It is named for the San Francisco peninsula, where it is well exposed. Attributes of this rock include its not being very strong—it has lots of elements like serpentine that are very slippery. It causes a lot of foundation problems for buildings and structures in those parts of the state where it is at the surface. Incidentally, Franciscan rocks underlie the south tower of the Golden Gate Bridge and were the subject of a great debate concerning the potential stability of that tower between Andy Lawson of Berkeley and Bailey Willis of Stanford, both of whom were very eminent geologists of their day, but seemed to enjoy disagreeing on almost everything.

In any event, I argued that instead of the slip being temporary and related to a past or forthcoming earthquake, it was occurring because in the areas of creep, one side of the fault had this very slippery rock. It turned out that where the creep zone stopped in the south, near Parkfield, was also where the rock type changed. So, in what was almost a pot-boiler and not intended as anything profound, I put forth this argument that creep was not temporal but had to do with the nature of the rock.

My suggestion started a lot of other people working on the problem. It also provoked a big debate right there at the Stanford meeting. The fellow who was debating me claimed that creep was premonitory to a great earthquake, and I responded, "Well, maybe during our lifetimes we will prove that, one way or the other." But that segment of the fault has not generated a big earthquake, and I think the weight of opinion now is that it probably never will, and that the rock types probably do have a lot to do with creep. The fault surface is not brittle and at least on one side there is slippery rock. Other people have done work on fluids that might be associated with creep. But here is a case where I tossed out an idea that proved to be a good one, important in trying to understand the mechanics of the overall San Andreas fault.

An interesting fallout of the discovery of creep on the San Andreas occurred shortly thereafter, when Frank Evison, an eminent New Zealand seismologist, was visiting Caltech and was concerned that perhaps creep was also occurring on the Alpine fault—New Zealand's analog to the San Andreas. He sought my advice on whether a geodetic (surveying) network might not easily detect the presence or absence of creep. My response was: "Oh hell, Frank, if you put in a geodetic network, it will cost you a fortune, it will have to be resurveyed periodically, and it will yield results that will inevitably be debated as to their statistical significance. Why not just build a concrete wall across the fault and see whether or not it cracks?" Well, that's exactly what he did on his return to New Zealand, at a locality on the Alpine fault near Springs Junction on the South Island.

I've since visited the locality several times and to this day, after some 30 years, there's not even a hairline crack in the wall [as of 2001]. In fact, it would have been difficult to build a concrete wall in that rainforest environment that didn't develop some cracks naturally. Because of the absence of any noticeable effects, the wall is sometimes know in New Zealand as "Evison's folly," although Frank himself jokingly refers to it as "Allen's folly!" Actually, I don't think it's a folly at all, inasmuch as we have documented the absence of creep on this segment of the fault cheaply and convincingly, and that's an important geologic observation.

1975 Paper on Evaluating Seismicity

Allen: I was president of the Geological Society of America from 1974 to 1975. The president was expected to give an address at the end of his term, hopefully of a scientific nature. My 1975 paper was published the following year, in 1976. What I did was summarize a lot of my ideas about how understanding geology and geologic criteria can help us in evaluating seismicity and seismic hazard. The paper had lots of illustrations drawn from areas around the world, such as Turkey, the Philippines, Japan, New Zealand, and so forth, demonstrating the relationship between seismicity and faults that have been recognized. To some degree, even if we arrived anew on the Earth today and did not know anything about its seismicity or earthquake history, if we had some good aerial photographs and satellite images, we could—by noting visible faults—draw some pretty firm conclusions as to where seismicity was likely to be found.[31]

This paper is widely quoted even today. Some people would say that I helped get the whole era of neotectonics and paleoseismology started, where people look at features of faulting in trying to understand their significance in relation to seismic hazard. I certainly was not the first,

however. The first study of this type along the San Andreas fault was done by Bob Wallace of the USGS, back in the 1940s in the Palmdale area—done, incidentally, as his Caltech Ph.D. thesis. But my 1975 paper brought together evidence from many parts of the world, including results of field studies that I had carried out in areas such as Turkey and Japan that had not been published independently.

I do not regret anything I said in the paper, although I do wish I had expressed some things differently. I said that virtually all large earthquakes in southern California had occurred on faults that *had* been, *could* have been, or *should* have been recognized by geologists prior to the earthquakes. I think the statement is still a good generalization, although instead of "virtually all" I should have said "most," because subsequently we have seen a number of earthquakes on blind thrust faults that do not reach the earth's surface. That was something we did not fully recognize at the time I was writing. In fact, Frank Press and I did a study recently that revealed that prior to about 1971, strike-slip faulting parallel to the San Andreas fault dominated the seismicity of southern California, whereas since that time, thrust faulting—much of it on blind thrusts—and faulting on faults *not* parallel to the San Andreas has dominated. We don't know why the change occurred.[32]

Although, in retrospect, I see that I could have written the seismicity paper a bit differently, my major point stood. For many years, seismologists thought they were the only ones who

---

31. Allen, C.R., "Geologic Criteria for Evaluating Seismicity," *Geologic Society of America Bulletin.* Vol. 86, p. 1041-1057, 1976.

32. Press, F., and Allen, C., "Patterns of Stress in the Southern California Region," *Journal of Geophysical Research.* Vol. 100, p. 6421-6430, 1995.

could really be of significant help in estimating seismic hazard. What I was trying to show was that geology provided equal and perhaps even more insight. Since that time, I think the record shows that geology is fully as important as seismology in the quantitative assessment of seismic hazard—the kind of thing we are trying to do in making seismic zoning maps, for example. And I think that my 1975 paper helped lead the way in this regard.

1976 Article on Earthquake Prediction

Allen: In 1976, the year following my presidency of the Geological Society of America, I was president of the Seismological Society of America, and they too expected a presidential address. The result was a rather short article titled "Responsibilities in Earthquake Prediction." This was not really a scientific article like the others I have been discussing here, but had to do with scientific behavior. At the time there was a lot of enthusiasm for earthquake prediction, many studies were underway, and I thought some things were being done that were a bit irresponsible.[33]

When you start talking about earthquake prediction, you immediately get the public's interest, and rightfully so. My talk was not really on science policy, but tried to point out some of the responsibilities of scientists involved in such studies. For example, I tried to define what an earthquake prediction should be. It should specify a time window in which the

---

33. Allen, C.R., "Responsibilities in Earthquake Prediction," *Seismological Society of America Bulletin.* Vol. 66, p. 2069-2074, 1976.

earthquake might occur and the prediction still be considered successful. It should specify the magnitude range and the area range. It should also give some indication of the author's confidence in the prediction. Merely predicting a magnitude 2 earthquake in southern California tomorrow is a truism. Predicting that a magnitude 6 earthquake will occur in southern California tomorrow is much different, especially if a particular area is specified. These are the kinds of things we should be careful about in promulgating a prediction and working with the public. That article has also been quoted a good deal. Hiroo Kanamori, former director of the Seismological Laboratory here at Caltech, keeps referring back to it.

Scott: By the mid-1970s the idea of achieving some fairly useful form of earthquake prediction was getting fairly strong play. Some people seemed to think that a fairly high degree of success was just around the corner—at least that was my impression.

Allen: Yes. I think at that time we were about at the peak of the curve of optimism.

Scott: In fact, the optimistic psychology of the time probably had a good deal to do with the funding of the NEHRP program begun under the law enacted in 1977, don't you think?

Allen: There is no question about that. I was involved, Frank Press was involved, and many others were involved in committees trying to get money into earthquake hazard assessment. The excitement was over prediction, but I think many of us had in the back of our minds the hope of getting better quantitative understanding of the probabilities of future earthquakes, not just short-term predictions. In retrospect we have to acknowledge being overly optimistic—grossly over-optimistic—about the expectations of earthquake prediction in the short-term sense, in the sense that the public had come to expect. In fact, it may be a long time, if ever, before we can make predictions on the basis of short-term precursors—dogs barking, a fault slipping, or something like that. When I say "short-term," I mean something on the order of hours, days, or weeks, whereas long-term probabilistic statements are typically based on something like 30-year expectations.

In trying to attract public attention and funding, some rather irresponsible statements were being made that perhaps went beyond the bounds of scientific integrity. My 1976 article asked several questions, one being, "If after a few years the program is really not successful, will we have the courage to admit it to ourselves and to our funding agencies?" Basically, I think that is what we have had to do, at least with respect to short-term prediction, which I again emphasize is what the public associated with the word "prediction." Such as: "Tomorrow afternoon at 4:00 there will be a big one in Los Angeles." Some of the scientists have sort of wiggled out by saying, "Well, by prediction I mean anything within the next hundred years." That is not quite fair, because that is not what the public thinks a prediction is.

Scott: It is certainly not what all the public discussion was about. In fact, for a time, 15 or so years ago [interview in 1996], the public had probably come to think that, in the relatively near future, we might actually be making reasonably accurate predictions of earthquakes shortly before they happened.

Looking Back at Earthquake Prediction

Scott: With the wisdom of hindsight, what are your retrospective thoughts on the earthquake prediction efforts?

Allen: For a long time the public has thought of earthquake prediction as seismology's main goal, although most seismologists would not consider prediction to be a major goal of seismology. But certainly the question "When can we predict earthquakes?" has long been in the public mind. And there were some predictions made. Charlie Richter once made a very outspoken statement, saying that earthquake prediction was basically for charlatans. At the time, I think his statement was fundamentally true, at least as applied to anybody who was then claiming to predict earthquakes.

I do not, however, think that Charlie's statement demonstrated much vision for the future, because I think that earthquake prediction is indeed something that someday will probably come to pass, to a much greater extent than is the case today. It has been a constant battle in recent years, however, trying to convince the public that, no, we cannot, as yet, predict earthquakes—particularly after we gave them such a buildup for prediction only a few years ago. And when these crackpots come along who *do* claim to be predicting earthquakes, we have big public relations problems. Also, in recent years not all of them have been crackpots; there have been reputable scientists who have made generalized predictions of various sorts. But there are still a lot of crackpots out there who are willing to say things like, "Tomorrow afternoon at five o'clock something terrible is going to happen."

The earthquake prediction effort got a big stimulus from Chinese claims, particularly during the Cultural Revolution, that they were, in fact, predicting earthquakes. Not only the scientists, but also people out in the farmyards and the countryside were using various sorts of techniques allegedly to predict earthquakes. This fitted in very nicely with Mao's philosophy that all wisdom rested with the broad masses of the people, so it should be no surprise that the people should be able to predict earthquakes. The program got a lot of political support for that reason. During the Cultural Revolution a lot of money and effort went into earthquake prediction efforts, particularly with schoolchildren and lay people.

It turned out, of course, that a lot of that Chinese effort was not scientifically well grounded, although some elements of it probably did have some scientific basis. The Chinese claims did, however, increase earth scientists' interest in earthquake prediction worldwide—"If the Chinese can predict earthquakes, why can't we?" American scientists looked very carefully at some of the Chinese efforts, and some things were worth looking at—particularly reported changes in groundwater levels observed before earthquakes. I participated in perhaps the earliest American visit to China in this regard.[34]

About 20 years ago, [interview in 1996] seismologists in this country developed some optimism that we really might have some success in earthquake prediction, and a good deal of effort was put into programs such as radon measurements and things of that sort. But there were also still

---

34. Press, F., Allen, C.R., et al., "Earthquake Research in China," *Eos*. Vol. 56, p. 838-881, 1975.

skeptics—I don't think Charlie Richter ever did think prediction merited such interest. In retrospect, however, I must say that we were overly optimistic then, and I include myself and a lot of other scientists. We were over-optimistic that earthquake prediction—in the short-term sense, that is, predicting an earthquake tomorrow or next week—was really within our grasp.

To this day, we still are not able to do that kind of prediction, although I am nevertheless optimistic that some day we will be able to do so. If you take a stick and bend it until it breaks, before the final break occurs there are a lot of little tell-tale clues that something is getting ready to happen. One of the problems with earthquakes is that they differ greatly one from another in the mechanics of what is going on down there underneath the ground. So, what may be true for one earthquake may not be true for another.

If we can predict some earthquakes, but not others, and unless we have a fairly high success ratio, it is not worth springing on the public as being in their interest. If, say, we are only 25 percent sure of the outcome of a prediction, then you would get the public worked up a lot of times when nothing happens afterwards. Some people in the engineering community have argued that earthquake prediction is not of any real social value anyway, because they say there is not much you can do beforehand even if you know that an earthquake is coming tomorrow, and the panic caused would outweigh any beneficial results of the prediction.

Scott: Yes, a prediction would need a good deal of reliability for us to make it a really useful policy tool. In California, particularly southern California, we went through a period of perhaps a decade when a lot of effort was devoted to trying to get ready for earthquake prediction. Getting public agencies and the public ready to deal with real earthquake predictions was a major goal of SCEPP, the Southern California Earthquake Preparedness Project. Work was done on such questions as what kinds of warnings should be issued, and in what circumstances.

Allen: The idea of earthquake prediction had a certain appeal to funders as something that might be practical, and a lot of work has been done on the problem. The national government and California each set up an Earthquake Prediction Evaluation Council—I initially chaired the federal one—to advise public agencies on the scientific legitimacy of any given prediction. The great bulk of predictions offered have had no scientific basis, but when predictions come along and make headlines, officials need some advice on their credibility. Is this another crackpot, or is it somebody who has some scientific legitimacy?

Scott: I think the federal and the California earthquake prediction evaluation efforts have performed a very useful service and have done a lot of good.

Allen: Yes, I think so, partly because they deflated a number of ill-founded predictions that otherwise would have drawn even more public attention. Also, part of our earlier enthusiasm about the earthquake prediction program has paid off, in the sense of what we call "long-term prediction." Although they are still in the category of research, we are able to make statements that certain areas are more

dangerous than others, and statements on the probability of an earthquake in a certain area within the next 30 years or 50 years.

We recognize that some faults are more active than others, and certain parts of California along the San Andreas fault have a higher hazard than other areas that may have faults, but faults with a much lesser degree of activity. This kind of information has been used quite legitimately in planning exercises and in setting priorities. For example, given a certain amount of money to retrofit highway bridges, which are the most critical to be retrofitted first? Those are legitimate questions to ask, and I think we have been giving some helpful answers.

In a sense, this partly came out of the earthquake prediction effort. Although admittedly in the public mind, prediction is still about something that is going to happen at 5:00 tomorrow afternoon, rather than a probabilistic statement about the likelihood of earthquakes in years to come. While we have been disappointed at our lack of success at *short*-term prediction, I think we should be very pleased with our progress on *long*-term earthquake prediction. Many scientists would rather say that these are long-term "forecasts" to avoid use of the word "prediction" for such probabilistic statements. There are now field studies of faults, where we are able to say something about the relative degrees of activity of different faults, how often they might break, and what kinds of earthquakes might occur, in terms of their magnitudes.

To sum up, prediction has been a mixed bag, some results not so good, but also some good results. It has been difficult dealing with the news media on earthquake prediction, especially television, where the networks want a story tonight. One of the famous predictions here in this area was the so-called Minturn prediction by a person who claimed to have an engineering background. He predicted, perhaps 20 years ago, an earthquake for Los Angeles during a certain time period, and the television stations made a great ballyhoo out of this. Minturn claimed to have had a record of several successful predictions over the previous few years. The television stations repeated these claims as if they were true, and it was the *Los Angeles Times* that blew the story apart, after some investigative reporting. They found the claims he had made were simply not true, and many of them were absurd. It was a major newspaper that had the time and put in the deliberate effort to get to the bottom of the story. All the TV people seemed to care about was getting something for the day's 6:00 pm news.

Scott: As we suggested earlier, the public's fascination with prediction back 20 and more years ago, probably had a good deal to do with developments such as passage of the Cranston Bill that set up NEHRP in 1977, as well as getting the whole earthquake program financed at substantially higher levels than before.

Allen: Yes, I think it did. Frank Press also worked very hard on that. He, like myself, was one of those who thought that earthquake prediction was—as it still is—a legitimate and promising scientific venture. Some engineers were disappointed because they believed that, in terms of the overall problem of earthquake hazards, too much money was going into the scientific end of it, especially to the earth sciences, as compared with what was going into relevant engineering studies. The engineers' argument had merits, although the earth scien-

tists had their act together somewhat better than the engineers in terms of working with the agencies in Washington, D.C. It's probably an historical accident, but the earth sciences community is well and very competently represented in the federal structure by the U.S. Geological Survey, whereas the engineers have no one agency in Washington to be an effective spokesperson for their interests.

I think that has since changed, particularly in that these recent disastrous earthquakes have resulted in a lot of additional funds being given to engineering studies. The engineers have come together better than before, and EERI is one organization that has tended to bring them together among themselves, as well as together with earth scientists, social scientists, etc. There seems to be much less jealousy and backbiting than there used to be.

1980 Paper on Reservoir-Triggered Earthquakes

Allen: Around 1980, an article I wrote on reservoir-induced earthquakes and engineering policy was published in three different places. It was first given as a paper at an international conference in Ohrid, Yugoslavia (now in the Republic of Macedonia), subsequently published again in Mexico, and also reprinted by the California Division of Mines and Geology. The California publication is probably the most accessible. This article was one of the publications in which I interacted with the engineering community.[35]

---

35. Allen, C.R., "Reservoir-Induced Earthquakes and Engineering Policy," *California Geology.* Vol. 35, p. 248-250, 1982.

There were several questions. First, was there really such a thing as a reservoir-induced earthquake? As I mentioned earlier, we now like to use the term "reservoir-triggered" rather than "reservoir-induced," because we recognize that such events represent the release of tectonic strain that was already there and whose release has simply been triggered by the presence of the perturbing reservoir. You'll recall that we talked about this subject earlier in connection with studies at Aswan High Dam, Egypt, but let's be more general here.

Some engineers and dam owners had stated—and some may still believe—that reservoir-triggered earthquakes do not, in fact, exist. I argued in the 1982 paper that, at the very least, engineers and owners had in some cases tended to "close their eyes" to the problem. I think that by this time there can be little doubt but that reservoir-triggered earthquakes have occurred, and most engineers now agree with that statement. Some of the earthquakes have been damaging, verging on disastrous. But we also have to recognize that there have been many debatable occurrences, where one might legitimately argue that the earthquake would have occurred even in the absence of the reservoir.

Scott: When you say the engineers and owners closed their eyes, do you mean they thought it would not happen?

Allen: I think they wanted to assume it would not happen.

Scott: An engineer or owner working under such an assumption would risk failing to design the dam for an earthquake that might, in fact, be triggered?

Allen: That's right. I made the argument in the 1982 paper that we had already seen some correlations of the biggest earthquakes that were suspected to be reservoir-triggered. These occurred in dams with deep water behind them, and in very large reservoirs. I made the argument that any dam built anywhere in the world in any geologic environment that would store water over some 300 feet deep should be designed on the assumption that a reservoir-triggered earthquake of a modest magnitude of 5 or 5.5 might occur. Some engineers took exception to that. Also, I suspect that it is not a terribly great design restriction, because dams are basically pretty stable structures anyway.

I believe, however, that most people now agree that there are reservoir-triggered earthquakes, and that they occur in all sorts of geologic environments. We cannot really say that they are more likely in granite than in sandstone. They may represent earthquakes that would have happened eventually anyway, but their arrival was certainly hastened by the dam and reservoir.

Scott: Are they all in areas that are known to have some seismicity?

Allen: No, they are not. That is an interesting point. A couple of reservoirs in South Carolina have had thousands of small earthquakes that were associated with the filling of very shallow reservoirs in areas of quite low natural seismicity. One of the moderate earthquakes occurred in the Canadian Shield, in Quebec, in rocks where there never had, historically, been major earthquakes. That was part of the argument—we could not at this time say that the absence of previous earthquakes proved you could not have a reservoir-triggered event.

In areas like California, of course, we were in pretty good shape because it clearly is a seismic area—there are enough highly active faults here so that almost any dam would be designed for earthquake shaking anyway. The main impact was on areas that were not known to be seismic. For example, as I mentioned before, I spent some time at Aswan High Dam in Egypt. In 4,000 years of human history in this area, there had never been a felt local earthquake until the ones in 1981 that we judged to be reservoir-triggered, for reasons discussed earlier.

Something we subsequently discovered that was not included in the 1982 article was that most or all of the *largest* reservoir-triggered earthquakes were in areas where there was some evidence of Late Quaternary (geologically recent) faulting. This turned out to be the case at Aswan. There is a fault there that had not been recognized, and that had no activity on it for at least 4,000 years, but it had some earthquake activity maybe tens or hundreds of thousands of years earlier.

Scott: Are you basically saying that all or almost all of the largest events involving dams and reservoirs are associated with some kind of active fault in the vicinity?

Allen: Yes, apparently so. The largest one was in Koyna in India, and after the event it was discovered that there was an active fault that passed through one arm of the reservoir. Oroville Dam has an active fault that goes right through the reservoir. Another of the biggest ones was at Xinfengjiang in China, and there is a major Quaternary fault very close to the dam.

I think that kind of knowledge is helpful now. Reservoir-triggered earthquakes can occur anywhere, but *large* reservoir-triggered earthquakes that are capable of doing substantial damage to a dam are apparently limited to areas of what we call Late Quaternary faulting—faults active in the past few tens to hundreds of thousands of years. That is of considerable help in identifying areas where special care may have to be taken in the design of projected large dams.

Scott: Could a dam and reservoir initiate a fault where none had existed before? Or is that pretty much out of the question?

Allen: I suppose it is possible, and of course all faults have to begin somewhere, even if it is only just a small crack in the ground. But generally speaking, I think the weight of the reservoir would not in itself be sufficient to induce new fault, although it can redistribute the stresses. Thus, the likelihood of a "new" fault generating a significant earthquake is generally considered vanishingly small. It is now thought that reservoir-triggered earthquakes occur for one of two reasons. First, the weight of the water may deform the rocks and cause some redistribution of stresses, which may lead to increased stress on a preexisting fault to the point where it breaks. Second, water may seep into cracks, go down into the earth, and actually lubricate faults that otherwise would not have moved at that time.

The first early demonstration that man can trigger earthquakes was at the Denver Arsenal in Colorado. Pumping water down a well at great depth triggered a lot of earthquakes, but the correlation was not recognized until eight years later. The pumping of water was the triggering event. Adding water to a fracture lubricates it, in a sense. So, a reservoir can do that, in addition to deforming the rocks.

The subject of reservoir-triggered earthquakes is very interesting, and there is still a great deal of ignorance about it. While reservoir-triggered earthquakes are rather rare—most reservoirs are filled without triggering any earthquakes at all—we cannot yet tell where they will happen and where they won't. How can we anticipate ahead of time what may happen—whether a reservoir will trigger earthquakes or not? So far we have not discovered any sure-fire means of doing that. The matter also raises interesting legal questions.

If you fill a reservoir and trigger even small earthquakes that would not have occurred without the reservoir, people living in the area will be concerned and may actually suffer some minor damage to houses. Are you, as the builder of the dam, then responsible? You could argue that the earthquakes are related to tectonic stress, and the earthquake would have occurred sooner or later anyway. Nevertheless, if the presence of the reservoir hastened the occurrence of an earthquake, that perhaps makes you liable.

Scott: Has what we have learned had any effect on the design of dams? Has the evidence of dam and reservoir-triggered earthquakes prompted the engineering community to be considerably more cautious in their dam design?

Allen: I would not say *considerably* more cautious, because most dams are already pretty stable structures, and in the initial design you can make them stronger without tremendous addi-

tional cost. For example, the U.S. Committee on Large Dams (USCOL) recently prepared a document on reservoir-triggered seismicity that they will distribute to their members to try to make engineers more aware of the problem.

1984 and 1991 Papers on Seismicity in China

Allen: I was lead author of two articles having to do with studies of major fault systems in China and Tibet. One was published in 1984 on the Red River fault and associated faults in Yunnan, and the other was published in 1991 on the Xianshuihe fault in eastern Tibet. I've already talked a good deal about the second one. I am rather proud of both these papers because they represent pioneering studies in areas where active faults had not been studied in this kind of detail.

China has lots of active faults, and for the most part up to that time they had not been studied, certainly not in the way we have studied the San Andreas fault, in trying to understand the seismic hazard and the history of geologically recent displacements.[36,37]

---

36. Allen, C.R., Gillespie, A.R., Han, Y., Sieh, K.E., Zhang, B., and Zhu, C., "Red River and Associated Faults, Yunnan Province, China: Quaternary Geology, Slip Rates, and Seismic Hazard," *Geological Society of America Bulletin*. Vol. 95, p. 686-700, 1984.

37. Allen, C.R., Luo Zhuoli, Qian Hong, Wen Zueze, Zhou Huawei, and Huang Weishi, "Study of a Highly Active Fault Zone: the Xianshuihe Fault of Southwestern China," *Geological Society of America Bulletin*. Vol. 103, p. 1178-1199, 1991.

The two faults studied were both major strike-slip faults, like the San Andreas. We covered hundreds of miles in China and Tibet looking at those faults. Those studies represented just good hard field work under very interesting field conditions, working with Chinese geologists, living in small towns, and so forth. We also had to do a good deal of hiking and walking to look at the fault in eastern Tibet.

Scott: It must have taken a major team effort with a lot of field support to cover such a large territory under those conditions.

Allen: In China, you necessarily work as a team. The idea of an individual going out and doing some independent field work is not very realistic. Funding came from the U.S. Geological Survey and from the State Seismological Bureau of China. The Chinese support was terribly important because it provided logistical support that otherwise we would have had very great difficulty paying for or even arranging.

The six-member team consisted of three American investigators and three Chinese investigators, but when we got out in the field we seemed to have a cast of thousands. For example, when working in eastern Tibet we had to take quite a few Jeeps, all our own food, and all our own gasoline. We had to take army troops because there was still some political instability in the area. So, in a sense, they were expeditions. We were not living in tents, however, but staying in small villages or towns that had lodgings of a sort. These were very concentrated efforts, and the Chinese worked very hard. We worked every day from dawn to dusk.

In a sense, these were pioneering studies, in that large segments of both faults had not been

previously recognized, and we were using field techniques quite unlike anything that had been used in this area before. The work also represented a very satisfying interaction with Chinese geologists—my coauthors—who also spent time in the United States as part of the cooperating U.S.-China programs.

The whole experience was very educational for me—learning about an area that few Westerners had ever seen before. It was also educational for the Chinese, I would hope, in learning the modern techniques of looking at faults. After the Cultural Revolution, they were pretty far out of the scientific mainstream.

1996 Chapter on Earthquake Hazard Assessment

Allen: The last contribution I will mention is the book Bob Yeats, Kerry Sieh, and I wrote.[38] Each of us had responsibilities for particular parts of the book, and my principal contribution was the final chapter, "Seismic Hazard Assessment," although I also wrote parts of the chapter on "Seismic Waves," and I had responsibility for coordinating the various chapters. The book is really the first of its kind, in that nobody had previously brought together the various geological elements used in the study of earthquakes, with particular emphasis on field studies and on international coverage. Although it is already being used as a textbook in some university graduate courses, it may have a greater long-term impact as a general reference book, partly because of the breadth of coverage

---

38. Yeats, R.S., Sieh, K., and Allen, C.R., *The Geology of Earthquakes*. New York, Oxford University Press, 568 p.,1997.

and the myriad examples and illustrations drawn from the world over. I personally worked very hard to make the index complete, with more than 3,000 individual entries. We hope that it will have wide sales in the engineering community as well as among earth scientists.

I am really quite proud of my chapter, because it brings together a lot of my ideas—geological, seismological, and even from the public policy point of view—that bear on the assessment of seismic hazard. I summed up a lot of things that I have never said anywhere else, and a book gives you this kind of opportunity to do a somewhat philosophical summary overview. I even introduced a bit of humor—relevant, I hope—in several of the footnotes. The chapter includes some of the same thoughts that I brought out in my Distinguished Lecture to the Earthquake Engineering Research Institute (EERI) at its 1995 Annual Meeting, that was published in *Spectra* (see below). For the EERI audience, however, it was more general, whereas the book is focused on actual techniques of hazard assessment.

1995 EERI Address and *Spectra* Article

Scott: Say a little more here about the main themes of the 1995 EERI Distinguished Lecture that you just mentioned.

Allen: My EERI talk was, in a sense, a philosophical statement on ideas that I had developed over a number of years. Included, for example, were thoughts on probabilistic vs. deterministic approaches, about which I have been involved in discussions with many people for a long time. I tried to bring those ideas together in a lay, nontechnical language. The

talk was, of course, not given primarily to earth scientists, but mainly to engineers, social scientists, public policy people, and so forth. I also insisted that the *Spectra* article be printed in the same informal language that I had used in the presentation at the annual meeting.[39]

The editor suggested, "Why don't you put in some references?" But when you start putting in references, you start changing the whole style of a piece. So when working up the written copy for the article, I used informal language, and put in phrases like, "Well, . . ." and other informal phrases. That helps make it clear to the reader that it was a speech.

The article had three main themes: earthquake surprises, the challenge of blind thrusts, and probabilistic vs. deterministic approaches. Virtually every earthquake turns out to be a surprise in the sense that things happen that we had not expected. This is, I suspect, as true for engineers as it is for geologists and seismologists. From the seismological point of view, we now recognize that earthquakes are far more different from one another than we had previously thought, as, for example, in the physics of the rupture process.

I tried to point out that these findings are challenging some of our basic tenets, such as the concept of the elastic rebound theory that has been widely accepted since it was first put forward by Harry Fielding Reid following the 1906 San Francisco earthquake. I guess my principal thought is that we perhaps don't

---

39. Allen, C.R., "Earthquake Hazard Assessment: Has Our Approach Changed in the Light of Recent Earthquakes?" *Earthquake Spectra*. Vol. 11, p. 357-366, 1995.

know as much as we thought we did about many fundamental aspects of earthquakes, and we must keep this in mind, particularly in hazard assessments. But it also means that the science still has some exciting times ahead.

Recent earthquakes, particularly in southern California, have pointed up the fact that blind thrusts are a more common cause of earthquakes than we had previously thought. Merely studying faults that break the earth's surface—however important—is not in itself enough to fully understand seismic hazard in many regions. There's a tremendous challenge in trying to identify and quantify the hazard from buried faults. I discussed a number of promising techniques, such as geomorphic studies of deformed geomorphic surfaces, and the use of GPS—Global Positioning System—data. Blind thrusts continue to be the subject of considerable scientific debate, but I think we are making progress.

Probabilistic vs. Deterministic Assessments

Scott: Say a little more about the probabilistic versus deterministic debate. Probability techniques are undoubtedly very important and instructive when used properly to help understand earthquake hazard levels. But sometimes I have an uneasy feeling that the probabilistic approaches can cantilever some major projections out from some pretty limited evidence, and I really don't know how much confidence should be placed in the results.

On the other hand, when you are dealing with complicated phenomena, and your evidence is limited and your understanding of the underlying physical processes is not as firm as you

would like, probabilistic approaches may be more useful than deterministic.

Allen: In my talk, I tried to emphasize that whichever approach you take—and the two approaches are not as necessarily different as some people might imagine—it basically goes back to judgment calls, which can be good or can be bad. When a judgment is put into a probabilistic approach, the answer will be no better than the judgment that went into it. On the other hand, when we talk about deterministic parameters like the "maximum credible earthquake"—a specific number, say magnitude 7.5—many people have not realized that a lot of judgment *also* underlies that seemingly hard number.

In fact, it may sometimes be difficult to go back and determine why such-and-such a specific number was chosen. Later if you were to ask me, "Why did you say 7.5?" I may have trouble defending that. In the probabilistic approach, if you can understand the mathematics, you can always go back and see where certain assumptions were made, and the results of making those assumptions. So, in that sense we call the approach "transparent," because at every step along the way where some specific judgment was made, that decision point can be recovered.

On the other hand, that probabilistic approach tends to fog the whole issue for many people, because the assumptions and judgments are sometimes buried in the mathematics. So it is certainly true that when one makes a probabilistic statement, the reader may say, "Well, with so much computerized gimmickry going into all this, why should I believe it?" But they also have every right to ask me why they should believe that 7.5 figure that I gave as a deterministic number.

Also, in an area like San Francisco, you are dealing not with just one fault, but with a number of faults. You really do have to have some sort of mathematical way of combining the hazards from different faults. If the Hayward fault can have a magnitude 6.9 earthquake, and the San Andreas fault can have an 8.1, then to quantify that as a hazard assessment for San Francisco, you need some way to pull those things together. Either fault could be the cause of a major earthquake that would affect San Francisco. One of the things the probabilistic approach allows you to do is to take several numbers and pull them together in a meaningful way—that is, to determine the overall hazard to an area like San Francisco from *all* the faults that might affect it, rather than concentrating simply on one individual fault.

The Building Seismic Safety Council (BSSC), an engineering and public policy group, is putting together new seismic zoning maps for the United States, and those maps are based, at least in part, on probabilistic approaches. The USGS is doing much of the hazard mapping—using some new and innovative probabilistic approaches—but engineers are participating in this and calling the shots on the hazard parameters of the final zoning maps. Perhaps for the first time, engineers, geologists, and seismologists are working together in producing such maps. The Federal Emergency Management Agency (FEMA) deserves credit for pushing and financing much of the project.

It is very easy to say that New Madrid, Missouri, has an earthquake problem, because it had great earthquakes there in the early 1800s,

and also to say that Los Angeles has an earthquake problem. But it is perfectly legitimate for engineers or public policy people to ask, "How do those two hazards compare?" If we need to know where to spend money on hazard reduction, or if an insurance company needs to make rate decisions, there is a need to know the *relative* probabilities of a damaging earthquake. We need something better than just to say, "Well, both areas can have big earthquakes." Knowing the maximum earthquake in each area is not very helpful in establishing what a reasonable insurance rate should be in each place.

Scott: You need to know something about the frequency of the earthquakes. They have been much more frequent in the Los Angeles area than in the New Madrid area.

Allen: Yes, in New Madrid we have only the one major historic group of large events to work with. But a lot of geologic evidence has begun to come to light that gives some idea how often such events have occurred there. The same is true of Charleston, South Carolina. Both areas have had only one historic event or group of events, but the geologic evidence is telling us about prehistoric events and how often they have occurred.

Chapter 9

Service on Local, State, National, and International Boards

*An interesting aspect of this activity
was that we occasionally came under
political fire.*

Local and State Boards

Scott: You discussed your service on the Consulting Board for Earthquake Analysis of the California Department of Water Resources. I believe you also served on some other state and local bodies set up in connection with earthquake-related problems.

Governor's Earthquake Council

Allen: Yes. For one thing, I served on the Governor's Earthquake Council, which in a sense was the predecessor to the Seismic Safety Commission. And I think we wrote a significant report.[40]

---

40. Stearns, J.G., Allen, C.R., et al., *First Report of the Governor's Earthquake Council*. Governor's Earthquake Council, Sacramento, California. 1972.

Scott: The Governor's Earthquake Council was set up by Governor Ronald Reagan at roughly the same time as the legislature set up the Alquist Committee, which a couple of years later recommended creation of the Seismic Safety Committee.

Allen: I served on the Earthquake Council, but never served on the Seismic Safety Commission, although I was asked to.

Scott: You were probably asked by several people. I remember asking you myself. When I was chairing the commission and a vacancy was coming up in earth sciences, I asked if you would be willing to serve.

Allen: Yes, and I told you I thought other and younger people ought to be getting involved. I am rather glad I am not on the commission now, because it seems to have become quite political.

Scott: Yes. Although they still seem to be doing some quite good work.

Allen: I think the leadership of Lloyd Cluff as chairman during a critical recent period has helped hold it together.

Liquefied Natural Gas Facility Review, and Post-San Fernando Report

Allen: The State Public Utilities Commission set up a board to advise it on the Liquefied Natural Gas (LNG) facility proposed to be located near Point Conception. That was sort of a one-shot job, not a long-continuing board.[41]

Scott: You also served on the commission set up by Los Angeles County after the San Fernando earthquake.

Allen: I was an alternate for Charlie Richter on that commission, and Harold Brown, president of Caltech, was the chairman. Harold asked me to help him on some things, and Charlie was a little unpredictable. But no, I was not very active on that Los Angeles County commission.

Only a few days after the earthquake, however, I was asked by the National Academy of Sciences to chair a panel to look at the initial lessons of the earthquake, and we wrote a report in—I think—record time, published long before the county commission's report, with some of the same conclusions. You'll recognize a number of still-active members of EERI who joined me on the NAS panel.[42]

State Mining and Geology Board

Allen: One additional state activity was my membership on the Mining and Geology Board, to which I was appointed by then-Governor Reagan—in 1969, I believe. This is the board that oversees the Division of Mines and Geology [now the California Geological Survey]. I served through 1975 and was chairman

41. Cluff, L.S, Allen, C.R., Degenkolb, H.J., Idriss, I.M., Jennings, P.C., and Johnston, R.G., *Seismic Safety Review of the Proposed Liquefied Natural Gas Facility, Little Cojo Bay, Santa Barbara County, California.* California Public Utilities Commission, Sacramento, California. 1981.

42. Allen, C.R., Bolt, B.A., Hales, A.L., Hamilton, R.M., Handin, J.W., Housner, G.W., Hudson, D.E., Kisslinger, C., Oliver, J.E., and Steinbrugge, K., *The San Fernando Earthquake of February 9, 1971: Lessons from a Moderate Earthquake on the Fringe of a Densely Populated Area.* National Academy of Sciences, Washington D.C. 1971.

of the board during the final year. In those years the board was more concerned with mining issues than with earthquake issues. But we pushed for a larger role by the division in earthquake-hazard assessment activities, which have now become a principal effort in the division's program. I recall that the Alquist-Priolo Act was just then being formulated, and even today I can recognize some of my own words—for better or for worse—in the detailed language of the act.

An interesting aspect of this activity was that we occasionally came under political fire. During the year in which I was chairman, the board went on record as supporting continued operation of a mine in Death Valley National Monument which was, I believe, the only producer in this country of a rare mineral critical to certain industries. The mine was in the mountains adjacent to the valley and out of sight to almost all visitors, but some environmental groups were very critical of the board, and I even recall an editorial in the *Los Angeles Times* that raked us over the coals.

National Efforts

Scott: I believe you were active on some review bodies for FEMA, and for the National Earthquake Hazards Reduction Program (NEHRP)?

FEMA-NEHRP Reviews

Allen: Yes, I have been deeply involved in the NEHRP programs and in trying to advise on those, where it has been possible to do so. I have also worked closely with the U.S. Geological Survey. I spent quite a bit of time on some of those groups. They were difficult assign-

ments, in that FEMA was trying to get advice on an integrated program, but the problem was that the USGS, representing the earth sciences community, was the only participating federal agency that was really competent technically. The engineers did not have their act together in any way that could feed money to the engineers the way USGS was pushing and supporting the earth science effort. Nor did the social science or public policy people have a unit like USGS. And, basically, FEMA itself was relatively incompetent back then. Now, however, things seem to have turned around.

Anyway, the whole thing became a little partisan—the engineers on the panels felt that the USGS was getting too much money. I can understand the engineers' frustration, because there was no government agency representing engineers, in a very competent way, like the Survey represented geology and geophysics. The Bureau of Standards wanted to think that it was the engineers' organization, but the engineers did not seem to agree. Also, of course, the National Science Foundation had a significant effort supporting earthquake engineering, but the nature of the NSF program seemed to be a subject of great debate among the engineers themselves.

Scott: What kinds of recommendations were made by the groups you served on?

Allen: We tried very hard to get FEMA to hire someone of international stature to head the NEHRP program, under FEMA's general umbrella, but they were never at that time able to work anything like that out. It was also a very difficult situation in that each of the participating government agencies, such as the

NSF and USGS, had its own autonomy and did not want to take orders from somebody else. And they particularly did not want to become subservient to an agency that they thought was relatively incompetent, at least for that particular job.

The problem also involved the organization of the government itself, and the peculiar position of the USGS as one of the few government agencies of really high competence, and how all that should be mixed together in carrying out the NEHRP program. In recent years, however, there have been much better relations among the various agencies and interests. And, I think, there has been an increasing realization that an effective national seismic hazards mitigation program has to be more broadly based than was initially envisaged, particularly perhaps by the scientists.

I must confess that I felt uncomfortable working on these FEMA-NEHRP panels. There were just too many hidden agendas present and power struggles going on—not only among the affected government agencies, but also among the various professional groups. I've concluded over the years that I wasn't born with the attributes of a hardball politician, and this sort of activity is simply not my cup of tea. While I enjoy arguing about what kinds of science and technology are important and needed, the question of who gets which part of the pie is much more of a political issue. Some very good things eventually came out of the NEHRP program, but I suspect they were more as the result of efforts by a few enlightened individuals than because of committee reports!

Scott: I can understand how participating in those panels might be frustrating. All things considered, we are probably lucky that quite a lot was accomplished under the NEHRP program, although more could have been done with better organization from the start. For the record, can I get you to identify the most important panels and their key publications, if any?

Allen: Two stand out. The first was the committee chaired by Karl Steinbrugge in 1970.[43] The second was the committee chaired by George Bernstein in 1993.[44] You'll recognize the names of many of the committee members as being—or having been—EERI stalwarts! I've also been on a number of other advisory groups, but, frankly, I can't remember them all, and in several cases I and others were "advisors" rather than contributing authors of the resulting reports.

Scott: You commented very favorably on the level of competence of the USGS. From its very beginning shortly after the Civil War, the

---

43. Steinbrugge, K., Allen, C.R., Degenkolb, H.J., Jahns, R.H., Newmark, N.M., Schoop, E.J., Shea, R.F., Stearns, J.G., and Wilson, J.T., *Report of the Task Force on Earthquake Hazards Reduction.* Office of Science and Technology Policy, Executive Office of the President, Washington D.C. 1970.

44. Bernstein, G.K., Allen, C.R., Andrews, R., Arnold, C., Beavers, J.E., Bertero, Davies, J.N., Davis, E., Jones, G.H., Pomeroy, P.W., Sharpe, R.L., Tierney, K.J., Tobin, L.T., and Whitman, R., *Report of the Advisory Committee of the National Earthquake Hazards Reduction Program (NEHRP).* Federal Emergency Management Agency, Office of Earthquakes and Natural Hazards, Washington D.C. 1993.

Survey had some remarkable, first-rate people. What do you think accounts for its ability to build up and maintain its status as such a unique agency of high scientific ability?

Allen: This is a question that has intrigued me over the years, although I have never been a full-time Survey employee. I think it's due to three primary factors: First, the USGS has a long-lasting tradition of scholarly excellence and hard work that goes back to the early leadership of men like John Wesley Powell and G.K. Gilbert. Tradition *does* make a difference in maintaining a high esprit de corps.

Second, partly owing to its relatively focused mission in geologic and topographic mapping, as well as in the collection of water resource data, the Survey has pretty well been able to isolate itself from political pressures from The Hill. To this day, insofar as I am aware, the only political appointee in the USGS is the director, and successive presidents have honored (until very recently) the long-time tradition of appointing the director from a list of scientifically qualified nominees submitted by the National Academy of Sciences.

Third—and most important in my opinion—is the tradition that almost all administrative leaders in the Survey, such as branch chiefs, are *rotated* every few years, so that former administrators then rotate back down into the ranks. This tradition has led to continually renewed vitality and has largely prevented what has happened in so many government agencies—even universities—that the "dead wood" has gradually risen to the top and stayed there.

Scott: Those are pretty much the same factors that Bob Wallace singled out in his oral

history interviews, basing his conclusions on his lifetime career in the USGS. But do you fear that political developments in recent years may be endangering these long-standing traditions?

Allen: I think what has changed in recent years is that drastically reduced budgets, as well as increased emphasis on projects with short-term practical payoffs, have seriously endangered the vitality of the Survey, particularly by almost eliminating the addition of *young* scientists, who represent the lifeblood of any research organization. Many of our universities now face the same problem.

Scott: I guess, it is a matter of maintaining a good balance between "basic" research, and "applied" research that has those practical payoffs. A few minutes ago you emphasized the unique and valuable contribution of the USGS to the BSSC seismic zoning maps, which represents what is essentially an applied science endeavor.

Allen: You're right, Stan. And I applaud this effort by the Survey to integrate its activities with those of engineers and public officials in trying to solve an important societal problem. But what I fear is that the basic research by the USGS that necessarily supports this and similar efforts will gradually be lost. This basic research has traditionally been a major contribution of the USGS, albeit somewhat in competition with the universities. But that competition has been healthy and productive. And much of the earth science research in the universities has even been funded by the Survey!

85

National Earthquake Prediction Evaluation Council

Allen: When the National Earthquake Prediction Evaluation Council (NEPEC) was set up, I believe in 1979, I served as its first chairman for some five years. NEPEC was established to advise federal agencies—and anyone else who wanted to listen—on the judged validity of earthquake predictions that had been offered, whether by "kooks," by well-meaning amateurs, or by reputable scientists. The need had become apparent earlier, when several very debatable predictions were promulgated and publicized by the news media. But potentially affected agencies at the federal, state and local levels had no formal way of independently verifying whether there was any scientific credibility to them. Should they or should they not react?

Fortunately, NEPEC had very little "business" during my tenure as chairman, but one episode in 1981 did cause quite a fuss. Two scientists, one from the U.S. Bureau of Mines and one from the U.S. Geological Survey, promulgated a very specific prediction of a great earthquake—magnitude 9.9!—just offshore of Peru, not far from Lima. Neither of the two agencies themselves endorsed the prediction and seemed, on the contrary, a bit embarrassed. Nevertheless, they were anxious not to appear to "muzzle" their employees, both of whom were reputable scientists. In time, the prediction became known as the "Brady-Spence prediction" after the two scientists who offered it.

The prediction was complicated by the fact that two U.S. government scientists were predicting a potential disaster in a foreign country, which muddied the water considerably and got the State Department deeply involved. The newspapers in Lima made a great ballyhoo out of the prediction, and near-panic existed in Lima as the date of the predicted event approached. Finally, the President of Peru formally requested the U.S. government to advise on the validity of the prediction, and the request quickly filtered down to NEPEC.

NEPEC faced a difficult challenge, inasmuch as most of the details of the prediction methodology had never been put down in writing by the promulgators, and both the predicted date of the big event and the alleged prediction methodology were somewhat of moving targets—that is, they kept changing. NEPEC met in Denver for two days in late January of 1981. TV cameras were in abundance, and an audience of perhaps 200 people—many from the press—was in attendance. After many frustrating hours of presentations and questions, NEPEC concluded that the prediction had no scientific validity. And no significant earthquake has occurred in the area to this day—some 20 years later.

An interesting postscript is that the episode was the subject of an exhaustive book by Richard Olson, a political scientist who is, incidentally, the brother of EERI-member Bob Olson. It includes many quotations attributed to me, since I chaired the "execution." Olson's book discusses many intriguing complications, such as the involvement of the State Department and the Office of Foreign Disaster Assistance, as well as the activities of a number of individuals in Peru. His treatise is not exactly complimentary to NEPEC or to me, but I can only comment that NEPEC's judgment regarding the validity of the Brady-Spence prediction turned out to be 100 percent right![45]

International Activities

Allen: In terms of international earthquake-specific matters, most of the time I spent in foreign countries involved research, rather than participation on international advisory committees. I have tended to shy away in recent years from such activities—particularly those sponsored by UNESCO—because they tend to get so bureaucratic and political. One seems to spend all one's time going to meetings and writing recommendations that no one pays much attention to.

UNESCO Activities

Scott: I believe you did, however, go abroad on some UNESCO activities, did you not?

Allen: I have participated in some international meetings, such as the Ohrid conference in Yugoslavia, which was a UNESCO affair. And I spent some time in the Balkan states as part of a UNESCO mission trying to help integrate seismic hazard issues in the Balkans. That one got a little political because Russian advisors were also involved, and at that time—and even today—the Russian and American approaches to seismic hazard assessment were very different. The Russian approach was much more mathematically oriented, whereas ours was more geologically oriented. We got into some political-type controversies that I did not particularly like. The outcome was that we all wrote reports, and probably nothing happened. But I did learn a lot from talking to scientists and seeing lots of earthquake geology—over a period of

some two months—in Turkey, Greece, Yugoslavia, Bulgaria, and Romania. And, hopefully, they learned something from me.

I do have to admit that UNESCO succeeded in getting lots of scientists from different countries to talk to one another—people who would not otherwise have done so. For example, seismologists from Greece and Turkey actually met and communicated with each other, under UNESCO auspices. I was also at a UNESCO-sponsored meeting in Algiers, where the informal communication between earthquake scientists from various North African countries was obviously beneficial.

China Committee

Allen: I almost forgot to mention the most important and rewarding international committee work in which I have been involved, that of the Committee on Scholarly Communication with the People's Republic of China (CSCPRC), which I'll hereafter refer to as simply the China Committee. I was active in CSCPRC activities for some 15 years.

The China Committee was set up in the early 1970s to try to establish contacts with scholars in China long prior to the time when the U.S. established formal diplomatic relations with the People's Republic. Although housed in, and administered by, the National Academy of Sciences (NAS), it was jointly sponsored by the NAS, the Social Sciences Research Council, and the American Council of Learned Societies. Particularly in the years prior to the establishment of diplomatic ties, the CSCPRC was one of the very few organizations with solid contacts with the community of scholars in China.

---

45. Olson, Richard S., *The Politics of Earthquake Prediction*. Princeton University Press. 187 pages, 1989.

For example, during the early 1970s, the China Committee sponsored a number of delegations of about ten people each in visits to China, and received several in return—in fields running the gamut from Chinese art history, to high-energy physics, to traditional Chinese medicine, to linguistics, to rice production, and so forth. About the only scholarly field that was verboten in the early days was that of the social sciences, because the Chinese apparently felt that the social sciences were a little too close to political policy, and that we might be prying into political rather than purely scholarly issues. Most of the science efforts were funded by the National Science Foundation, which at that time could not itself directly support work in China.

In 1974, I was appointed by the China Committee as vice chairman—Frank Press was the chairman—of a 12-person seismological delegation to look at the earthquake prediction effort in China, partly in response to Chinese claims of a number of successful predictions that I have alluded to earlier in these interviews. This was during the waning years of the Cultural Revolution, so it was a fascinating experience from a social-political, as well as from a scientific, point of view. Our scientific report was read with interest by many people, and while we were impressed with the general seismological efforts that were underway in China, we were somewhat "underwhelmed" by their actual claims of successes in prediction.

We visited a number of schools, for example, where the schoolchildren claimed to have made successful earthquake predictions based on measurements that were simply unbelievable, such as major daily changes of temperature at depths of a few feet in the ground. One had to admire the enthusiasm that the program engendered, but they were really kidding themselves about the scientific significance of much of the work.[46]

An interesting sidelight of this visit occurred while our group was in Beijing. On one day, our hosts gave us the option of visiting either Qinghua University—China's premier engineering school—or visiting a "May 7th Cadre School" in the countryside, where Chinese intellectuals had been sent (some never to return!) to experience the values of manual labor and to cogitate on the teachings of Chairman Mao. I chose to visit the Cadre School, which was a fascinating—indeed, frightening!—experience.

A number of years later, I met the president of Qinghua University when he was visiting Caltech, and I apologized for not visiting his university when I had the earlier opportunity, but instead chose to visit the Cadre School. His response was, "It wouldn't have made any difference. You would have seen essentially the same thing at either place!" China was a mind-boggling place to visit during the Cultural Revolution, but the changes in China since that time have *also* been mind-boggling.

I served on the China Committee [the equivalent of the Board of Directors], and also on several of its panels, from 1982 to 1989. The last year, 1989, I was chairman. I visited China several times under the aegis of the committee, and I chaired the American Plate Tectonics

---

46. Press, F., Allen, C.R. et al., "Earthquake Research in China," *Eos.* Vol. 56, p. 838-881, 1975.

Delegation in its visit to Tibet in 1979, as I mentioned earlier in these interviews.

Serving on the China Committee was particularly rewarding because the group was made up of eminent scholars from a wide range of disciplines—not just science. In some ways it was, in fact, a humbling experience for a scientist, and I developed great respect and admiration for the abilities and insights of my nonscientific colleagues. Perhaps, however, the most memorable occasion was, while serving as chairman, being the guest of honor at a banquet hosted by the Chinese minister of education at the Great Hall of the People in Beijing. I ate well!

One of the topics of discussion at that dinner, incidentally, had to do with the failure of Chinese graduate students who studied in the U.S. to return to China following graduation. Earlier, the Chinese government had made it diffi-cult for students to study abroad for this very reason. For example, they prevented spouses from leaving the country, in order to encourage their partners to return after obtaining their degrees. The minister recognized that the great bulk of Chinese students who came to the U.S. stayed here, but he said the government's policy had now changed and no longer discouraged students from leaving China.

He opined that "once a Chinese, always a Chinese," and that wherever they were in the world, they would tend to bring credit to their homeland. They would also retain great loyalty to the homeland—culturally if not political-ly—and eventually many probably *would* return, particularly as housing conditions and research facilities gradually improved in China. I thought it was a rather thoughtful statement.

Interdisciplinary Communication and EERI

I certainly didn't set out initially with any specific thought of bridging fences.

Scott: Would you talk a little about interdisciplinary matters? You have actively communicated with people in other disciplines and have done a good deal to promote interdisciplinary understanding in earthquake engineering and seismic safety. George Housner, for one, commented especially on your significant work in helping improve communication between scientists and engineers.

Improving Communication Between Disciplines

Allen: Well, I'm flattered that such remarks have been made. Yes, I have tried very hard over the years to improve the rapport between scientists and engineers, particularly with regard to establishing realistic seismic criteria for critical projects such as dams, aqueducts, and nuclear facilities. I think it is fair to say that both communication and mutual respect between the two groups are now a lot better than they were 40 years ago.

Scott: What were the principal causes of the earlier lack of rapport?

Allen: A large part of it seemed to stem from the perception that the two groups were stepping on each other's toes—in the sense that members of each group felt that members of the other group were sometimes making public statements and recommendations outside of their respective areas of competence. Geologists and seismologists, for example, were sometimes visualized as offering engineering judgments outside of their areas of expertise, in such fields as maximum building heights. Similarly, engineers were sometimes offering judgments on earthquake probabilities or fault relationships that were viewed by earth scientists as ill-advised. It must be recognized that then, much more than today, university faculties in the earth sciences were far more isolated from their engineering colleagues, and few students took courses in the counterpart fields.

Scott: What did you personally do to help change things for the better?

Allen: I certainly didn't set out initially with any specific thought of bridging fences. But, starting with my service on the Department of Water Resources Consulting Board for Earthquake Analysis, which I have alluded to earlier, I found myself fascinated with engineering projects and talking more and more with engineers. Partly as a result, I participated in many engineering meetings, often as an invited speaker, and my remarks seemed to be generally well received by the engineering community. I remember, for example, speaking at least twice to the Structural Engineers Association of Southern California about the geological-seismological aspects of regional earthquakes.

Gradually, I think, these interactions—and those of many others, of course—helped promote interdisciplinary understanding and mutual respect between earth scientists and engineers.

Another specific effort that I enjoyed was participating with the Caltech Earthquake Research Affiliates, which was a fundraising group that we set up at Caltech following the 1952 Kern County earthquake—supporting research work jointly in seismology and earthquake engineering. Members were mainly banks, utilities, insurance companies, etc., who often sent their chief engineers to annual meetings at Caltech.

On alternate years, we ran geological field trips to areas of particular earthquake interest, such as the Owens and Imperial Valleys, and I was often in charge. It was the first time that many of these engineers had seen faults and other earthquake features in the field, and it was clearly educational for them, as well as stimulating for me in talking with them about their companies' earthquake problems. I established many contacts with engineers through this program, many of which I retain to this day. Again, it was one more step in establishing mutual respect and understanding.

I don't mean to imply for a moment, however, that I developed real engineering expertise, or vice versa. In that connection, I recall one instance in which I was involved with geotechnical engineer and Cal professor Harry Seed, along with other experts on a multidisciplinary consulting team for a major engineering project. In discussing specific debatable issues, such as fault orientation near the proposed facility, Harry entered into the geologic discussions vigorously and productively. When, however, it came time to vote on the weighting of the specific geologic parameters to be entered into the logic tree analysis, Harry declined to participate.

When I asked him why, he said that if *he* voted on the geologic issues, *I* might wish to vote on the strictly engineering issues! He said this with complete respect, but it reflected his rightful concern that expertise be appropriately applied. Over the years I developed tremendous respect for Harry Seed's judgment, and his untimely death was a great loss to the profession. He not only was a brilliant, imaginative, and productive engineer, but also was constantly concerned with professional ethics and broader issues.

Scott: Harry Seed served on the Seismic Safety Commission for several years when I was also a member. He was an extremely thoughtful and effective commissioner. Would you care to mention a few of the other earthquake engineers with whom you have been most interactive?

Allen: First and foremost among those has been—and still is—George Housner, who not only was my long-time colleague at Caltech, but also served together with me on the California Department of Water Resources (DWR) Consulting Board, and on numerous other boards and committees. He was not only a source of infinite wisdom and historical perspective, but also a man with truly remarkable patience in dealing with neophytes like myself. Nor has he hesitated to be critical—or at least respectfully skeptical—of earth scientists in some aspects of their participation in engineering projects.

It is difficult to single out other engineers with whom I have beneficially interacted because I will inevitably leave out important figures. But, offhand, let me particularly mention—in addition to Housner and Seed—Wallace Chadwick, Ray Clough, Ed Cording, Allin Cornell, Ed Idriss, Skip Hendron, Don Hudson, Paul Jennings, Bob Kennedy, Eric Kollgaard, Tom Leps, John Lowe, Robin McGuire, Ralph Peck, Jim Sherard, and Karl Steinbrugge. Most of these are, or have been, EERI members.

It would be unfair to mention engineers from whose knowledge and wisdom I have personally benefitted without also mentioning other earth scientists—geologists and seismologists—who have been major contributors to increased communication and understanding with earthquake engineers. Those particularly coming to mind are Hugo Benioff, Kelvin Berryman, Bruce Bolt, Lloyd Cluff, Kevin Coppersmith, Art Frankel, Tom Heaton, Dick Jahns, Bill Lettis, Leon Reiter, Kerry Sieh, Burt Slemmons, Paul Somerville, Carl Stepp, and Bob Wallace. There are, of course, many others.

EERI Activities

Scott: EERI has, of course, played a very important role in interdisciplinary communication, and you have already referred to EERI in a number of connections. Before we wind up this oral history, however, I hope you will say a few more words about your own EERI-related activities.

Allen: I was elected to membership in EERI in 1966, at a time when election was strictly honorary. I was, in fact, greatly honored to have been one of the few nonengineers elected to the very elite group. But, along with many other EERI members, I became convinced that elitism was not in the best interest of public service—as opposed to personal professional advancement—and I worked hard to make membership basically voluntary, as subsequently came to pass in 1973. In my opinion, EERI is a considerably stronger policy- and research-oriented organization as a result of this change.

I do not recall all the EERI committees on which I have served, but two stand out: I was elected to the board of directors in 1985-1988, and we faced many of the typical challenges of a rapidly growing professional organization, particularly in leadership, staffing, and definition of mission. And in 1995, President Loring Wyllie appointed me chairman of the nominating committee. I am particularly proud that we nominated the first representative of the social and behavioral sciences as president-elect (Joanne Nigg). The blending of disciplines in pursuit of a major societal problem has been a very unique attribute of EERI, and I hope I have contributed to it. No other professional organization of which I am a member has the broad multidisciplinary base that EERI has.

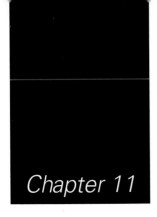

Chapter 11

Personal Notes

*Coastal Washington . . . is a very
different environment from that of
southern California, and by travelling
back and forth, I enjoy the best of two
quite different worlds!*

Scott: Before ending these interviews, would you care to say
a little more about your personal, nonprofessional life?

Allen: While I never married, I have stayed quite close to
my brother and sisters and their families. So in this regard I
have enjoyed some aspects of family life. And with no children
of my own, I have helped financially to put some of my neph-
ews and nieces through college.

I must say that, although I live alone, I am not a hermit-like
person, and I truly do enjoy being around other people. I look
forward to eating lunch with my colleagues at the Caltech
Athenaeum—our faculty club—and I have particularly enjoyed
leading trips for our Caltech Associates, who are major financial supporters. In recent years, I have led Associates trips to
New Zealand (twice), Tierra Del Fuego, the Colorado Rockies, the San Juan Islands and Olympic Peninsula, Mt. St.
Helens, Death Valley, the northern Cascades, the Mammoth
area, and the California Big Sur coast. These trips involve a lot
of preparatory work on my part but are a lot of fun and are

apparently enjoyed by the participants. I try to emphasize not only geology, but also local history, fauna and flora, and so forth.

Finally, I have gotten to know a number of people who live near me in a little enclave on the Washington coast where I built a second home, and I have enjoyed contacts up there. Coastal Washington, in the rainforest overlooking the rugged windswept Pacific coast, is a very different environment from that of southern California, and by travelling back and forth, I enjoy the best of two quite different worlds! Many people have asked why I chose coastal Washington, and I can only remind them that I not only did my undergraduate work in the Pacific Northwest, but also spent parts of seven summers doing glaciological field work on Mt. Olympus, only a few miles northeast of my second home near Copalis Beach.

Scott: What about hobbies, or musical and cultural interests?

Allen: I used to play the flute when I was young. But while I no longer play an instrument, I continue to enjoy music very much, and I am an avid fan of a great variety of types of music. I particularly like ragtime and country-and-western music, which some of my friends find surprising. Mozart is also a favorite, particularly his two flute concertos.

I still enjoy reading murder and spy mysteries, although they seem to have lost some of their best base material since the end of the Cold War. And I have enjoyed solving crossword puzzles as a good way to get your mind off business but still remain mentally challenged. Mainly as a result of my World War II experience, I am still fascinated by aviation, and I

subscribe loyally to *Aviation Week and Space Technology*. Again, harking back to my service as an aerial navigator during the war, whenever I fly I take my aeronautical charts along and seem to be one of the few business travelers who prefer a window seat! I rather pride myself on being able to look out of an airplane window anywhere in the country and have a pretty good idea where we are at the time. It's particularly challenging with partial cloud cover and at night, when one depends solely on patterns of city lights.

At least up until recently, when I've found it a bit difficult to get around, I have especially enjoyed trout fishing—fly fishing, that is. Together with colleagues from Caltech, particularly Paul Jennings, Bob Sharp, and Arden Albee, I have, over the years, backpacked into many delightful trout fishing areas in the Sierra Nevada and the Rockies. I mentioned earlier that several of us backpacked into all four corners of Yellowstone Park, where there's remarkably good fishing for cutthroats. And Paul Jennings and I have found some surprisingly good trout fishing in the mountains here in southern California—if you're willing to walk for an hour beyond the end of the road. Additionally, I have had the opportunity to drop a line into promising stream waters in Chile, Argentina, New Zealand, Tajikistan, and even Tibet. Alas, however, the beautiful mountain streams of eastern Tibet seem to contain no trout—only a variety of scaleless carp.

Scott: Finally, as a way of winding up these sessions, tell us something about the honors and awards received during your career that have meant the most to you.

Allen: I'm perhaps most proud to have been elected to both the National Academy of Sciences and the National Academy of Engineering. I would like to think that this is indicative of my broad interests and contributions in a wide variety of areas. Interestingly, both elections took place in the same year, 1976, although the two organizations are completely independent and have completely different nomination and election procedures. Insofar as I can find out, although I may be wrong, only three other EERI members are also members of both academies: Ray Clough, George Housner, and Jim Mitchell. I am also a member of the American Academy of Arts and Sciences, elected in 1974.

Several other awards are of particular significance to me. In 1994, I received the Alfred E. Alquist Award from the California Earthquake Safety Foundation, which was presented at EERI's annual meeting. I understand that it recognizes public service in contributions to the awareness and mitigation of earthquake hazards in California.

In 1995, I was designated as EERI's Distinguished Lecturer, which again represents, I think, perceived contributions in a broad spectrum of earthquake-related activities. Also in 1995, I received the Medal of the Seismological Society of America, which is not awarded every year and was a particularly great honor that came as an utter surprise to me. [Subsequent to this 1995-1996 series of interviews, in 2001 EERI awarded Allen the George W. Housner Medal, its most prestigious award.]

Yes, I have been amply rewarded and awarded, so to speak, and I feel immensely grateful to so many people—family, friends, and professional colleagues. And, as I've said several times in these interviews, it's all been fun!

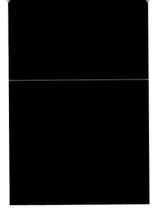

Photographs

Clarence R. Allen, 1991.

Allen (1st row, 2nd from right) with his fellow B-29 crew members, Okinawa, 1945.

Glaciological field studies on the Malaspina Glacier, Alaska, 1951.

Allen and geologist E. Gamus during fieldwork along the Philippine fault on the island of Leyte, 1962.

Lloyd Cluff and Clarence Allen during field studies of the Boconó fault, Mérida Andes, Venezuela, 1968.

Planetable mapping along the Atacama fault, northern Chile, in 1969. Allen (in helmet) and Caltech graduate student Walter Arabasz are flanked by Chilean colleagues.

Allen with Japanese geologists Atsumasa Okada (left) and Tokihiko Matsuda (right), Tokyo, 1969, following joint fieldwork on the Médian Tectonic Line, a major active fault of western Japan.

Clarence Allen and Karl Steinbrugge at the Taylor Winery, near Hollister, California, circa 1970. This is the locality where Karl Steinbrugge and Ed Zacher first recognized and documented gradual creep along the San Andreas fault in 1956.

103

Allen points out features of Caltech seismographic recordings to assistant Lind Gee and graduate student Stephen Cohn, circa 1978.

First meeting of the National Earthquake Prediction Evaluation Council, February 1980. Back row: David Hill, C. Barry Raleigh, Keiiti Aki, James Savage, Neil Frank, Neil Davis, Robert Engdahl, Robert Wallace. Front row: John Filson, William Menard, Clarence Allen (chairman), Robert Wesson, Clement Shearer (recording secretary).

Allen (third from right) with Pakistani colleagues on inspection tour of earthquake hazards at Tarbela Dam and Lake, 1981.

Fly-fishing for big browns on the Ruakituri River, New Zealand, 1986. (Photo by fishing partner Paul Jennings)

Allen (center) talks with Tibetan lama (foreground) about history of earthquakes along Xianshuihe fault, 1986.

Left to right: Caltech graduate student Zhou Whawei, Chinese geologist Luo Zhuoli, and Clarence Allen as guests at a local village wedding party, Tibetan plateau, 1986.

Left to right:
Ralph Peck,
Clarence Allen,
and Evert Hoek,
consulting panel
for the
remediation of
the Dutchman's
Ridge landslide,
near Mica Dam,
B.C., Canada,
1988.

Independent Board of Consultants, Metropolitan Water District Eastside Reservoir
Project (now Diamond Valley Lake). Left to right: Thomas Leps, I. M. Idriss, William
Wallace, Richard Kramer, Clarence Allen, Alan O'Neill, June 1993..

Allen explains the wall across the Alpine fault near Springs Junction, South Island, New Zealand to members of a Caltech Associates field trip in 1997. The 80-foot-long concrete wall was erected in 1964, at Allen's suggestion, squarely athwart the Alpine fault, in order to confirm or disprove the presence of ongoing creep along the fault. Now sometimes known as "Allen's folly," the wall hasn't shown a trace of cracking or deformation, at least through 2001!

Clarence Allen, Lloyd Cluff, and Ed Idriss sightsee in Jerusalem, 1999, while attending a meeting of the Technical Advisory Board for Israel Electric Corporation's proposed Shivta-Rogem nuclear power plant.

G

Gamus, E., 101

Garlock fault
    California Aqueduct, crossing of, 43

Gee, Lind, 104

Geological Society of America, Allen president
    of, 68

Geology
    relationship of geologic structures to
        earthquakes, 65–66
    seismicity, evaluating, 68–69
    See also Field work

Geomorphology, 20–21

Geophysics, 15, 17, 19–20, 27

Gilbert, G.K., 85

Glaciers
    Allen's early career studies of, 20–21, 62–63
    Blue Glacier, Washington, 62–63
    Malaspina Glacier, Alaska, 101
    mapping, 62–63

Global Positioning System (GPS), 79

Golden Gate Bridge, Franciscan rocks under,
    67

Governor's Earthquake Council, State of
    California, 82

Groundwater, expert witness testimony on, 42

Gutenberg, Beno, 22–23, 31, 39

H

Hayward, California fault, 80

Heaton, Thomas, 93

Heim, Albert, 33

Helmberger, Donald, 39

Hendron, Alfred J. (Skip), 53, 93

Hill, David, 104

Hill, Mason, 35

Hoek, Evert, 107

Hoover Dam, Nevada, 48

Hosgri fault, California, 56–57

Housner, George W., 25, 39, 42, 91, 93, 97

Housner, George W. Medal, Earthquake
    Engineering Research Institute (EERI),
    Allen recipient of, 97

Hudson, Donald E., 93

I

Idriss, I.M. (Ed), 51–52, 93, 107, 109

Iguaçú River, Brazil-Argentina, 49

India, Koyna Dam, 46, 48, 75

Indonesia
    earthquake (1926, 1946), 31–32
    Sumatra fault, 31–32, 34

Israel, Shivta-Rogem nuclear power plant, 109

Itaipu Dam, Brazil-Paraguay, 44, 48–49

Iwan, Wilfred D., 39

J

Jahns, Richard H., 20, 37–38, 93

Japan, Median Tectonic Line, 103

Jennings, Paul C., 7, 39, 93, 96, 105

K

Kamb, Barclay, 39, 63

Kanamori, Hiroo, 39, 69

Kennedy, Robert P., 93

Kern County, California earthquake (1952), 92

Kirschvink, Joseph, 39

117